How to Become

a High Value Man

Character vs Charisma

Camilet Cooray

Nathasha Publishers (Sri Lanka & The Philippines),
nathashapublishers@outlook.com

ISBN: 9798852186201

Cover design by Camilet Cooray for
Nathasha Creations (Sri Lanka & The Philippines)

First Edition: July 2023
Printed in the United States of America

Table of Contents

Introduction 1

The Man and His Car 2

The Life-Changing Nature of Decision Making 3

The Power of Desire 4

Welcoming All Experiences 5

The Power of Resolve 6

Persistence in Learning to Walk. 7

Discovering Life's Treasures 8

The Importance of Clarity in Decision Making 9

Embracing Responsibility for Decisions. 10

The Power of Small Decisions 11

Overcoming Decision Paralysis 12

Making Decisions Based on Values. 13

The Power of Intuition. 14

Seeking Wise Counsel 15

Embracing Failure as a Learning Opportunity. 16

The Art of Decision Refinement. 17

The Ripple Effect of Decisions. 18

Cultivating Patience and Trust in the Decision-Making
   Process. 19

The Impact of Fear on Decision Making. 20

Setting Clear Goals and Objectives. .21

The Art of Prioritization. 22

Avoiding Decision Overload 23

Developing a Decision-Making Framework. 24

Learning from Past Decisions 25

Considering the Short-Term and Long-Term Impact 26

Embracing Flexibility and Adaptability 27

The Power of Visualization 28

Trusting Your Instincts 29

The Role of Emotions in Decision Making 30

Seeking Diverse Perspectives 31

The Balance between Logic and Intuition. 32

The Power of Reflective Thinking. 33

Harnessing the Power of Information 34

The Art of Compromise 35

Embracing Uncertainty and Risk 36

The Impact of Decision Making on Others. 37

Learning to Let Go of Regret. 38

The Power of Decision-Making Skills 39

Cultivating a Growth Mindset in Decision Making. 40

Avoiding Analysis Paralysis 41

Understanding the Power of Timing 42

Balancing Short-Term Gratification with Long-Term Goals. . . . 43

Learning from Successful Decision-Makers 44

Applying Critical Thinking Skills. 45

Setting Realistic Expectations 46

The Power of Incremental Progress. 47

Seeking Continuous Feedback. 48

Embracing Decision-Making as a Journey 49

Emphasizing Ethical Decision Making 50

Evaluating the Long-Term Consequences. 51

Cultivating Emotional Intelligence. 52

Harnessing the Power of Data and Analytics. 53

Avoiding Decision Fatigue 54

Promoting Collaboration in Decision Making 55

Embracing Innovation and Creativity 56

The Importance of Self-Reflection 57

Recognizing the Power of Adaptation 58

The Role of Accountability in Decision Making. 59

Fostering a Culture of Decision-Making. 60

The Role of Intention in Decision Making 61

Developing Decision-Making Resilience 62

Embracing Decision-Making as a Learning Journey. 63

Applying Ethical Decision-Making Frameworks. 64

Balancing Rationality and Intuition 65

Leveraging Technology in Decision-Making. 66

Reflecting on Systemic and Societal Implications. 67

Balancing Confidence and Humility 68

Celebrating Decision-Making Successes 69

Navigating Ethical Dilemmas 70

Leveraging Emotional Intelligence in Decision Making. 71

Recognizing Bias in Decision Making 72

Embracing Diversity and Inclusion in Decision Making 73

Evaluating the Costs and Benefits of Decisions 74

Developing Decision-Making Rituals 75

Leveraging Decision-Making Tools and Models. 76

Practicing Mindfulness in Decision Making 77

Mitigating Decision-Making Biases 78

Striving for Ethical Leadership in Decision Making 79

Harnessing the Power of Intentional Decision-Making 80

Applying Decision-Making to Personal Relationships. 81

Balancing Logic and Emotion in Decision Making 82

Embracing Failure as a Steppingstone to Success. 83

Recognizing the Influence of Social and Cultural Factors 84

Empowering Others in Decision Making 85

Building Resilience in the Face of Decision-Making
    Challenges 86

Emphasizing Sustainable Decision Making 87

Engaging in Continuous Learning and Growth 88

Celebrating Decision-Making Independence 89

Balancing Short-Term and Long-Term Considerations. 90

Adapting to Changing Circumstances. 91

Recognizing and Mitigating Decision-Making Biases 92

Cultivating a Supportive Decision-Making Environment 93

Embracing Intuition as a Valuable Guide. 94

Learning from Others' Decision-Making Experiences 95

Using Visualization Techniques. 96

Evaluating the Opportunity Cost 97

Taking Responsibility for Decision Outcomes. 98

Celebrating the Decision-Making Journey 99

Leveraging Decision-Making in Team Settings 100

Evaluating Decision-Making Risks 101

Nurturing Ethical Decision-Making in Organizations 102

Embracing Decision-Making as a Driver of Innovation 103

Leveraging Decision-Making in Personal Growth. 104

Fostering Decision-Making Confidence 105

Incorporating Feedback Loops in Decision Making 106

The Role of Decision-Making in Crisis Management. 107

Balancing Decisiveness and Analysis 108

Embracing the Evolution of Decision-Making 109

Utilizing Decision-Making in Personal Finance 110

Embracing Decision-Making in Health and Wellness 111

The Impact of Decision-Making on the Environment 112

Cultivating Decision-Making in Education 113

The Role of Decision-Making in Entrepreneurship 114

Applying Decision-Making in Conflict Resolution 115

Decision-Making in Ethical Dilemmas in Medicine 116

Incorporating Decision-Making in Social Justice Advocacy 117

The Role of Decision-Making in Personal Relationships. 118

Cultivating Decision-Making in Parenting 119

Integrating Decision-Making in Project Management. 120

The Role of Decision-Making in Public Policy. 121

Balancing Personal and Professional Decision-Making 122

Decision-Making in Philanthropy and Social Impact. 123

The Role of Decision-Making in Crisis Communication. 124

Applying Decision-Making in Technology Development. 125

Decision-Making in Legal and Ethical Dilemmas 126

Incorporating Decision-Making in Supply Chain
    Management 127

Decision-Making in Mergers and Acquisitions 128

Cultivating Decision-Making in Scientific Research 129

Decision-Making in Human Resources Management 130

Applying Decision-Making in Risk Management. 131

Decision-Making in Project Prioritization. 132

Decision-Making in Sales and Marketing. 133

The Role of Decision-Making in Personal Productivity 134

Decision-Making in Quality Management 135

Applying Decision-Making in International Business 136

Decision-Making in Nonprofit Organizations 137

The Role of Decision-Making in Government Policies. 138

Decision-Making in Personal Time Management. 139

Leveraging Decision-Making in Supply Chain Optimization . . .140

Decision-Making in Organizational Change Management. 141

Applying Decision-Making in Crisis Response 142

Decision-Making in Customer Service Excellence 143

The Role of Decision-Making in Innovation Management 144

Decision-Making in Corporate Social Responsibility. 145

Leveraging Decision-Making in Financial Risk
Management 146

Decision-Making in Public Relations and Reputation
Management 147

Applying Decision-Making in Knowledge Management 148

The Role of Decision-Making in Business Ethics 149

Decision-Making in Cultural Sensitivity. 150

Leveraging Decision-Making in Data Analytics. 151

Decision-Making in Public Health Management 152

Applying Decision-Making in Disaster Preparedness and
Response 153

Decision-Making in Artificial Intelligence and Machine
Learning. 154

The Role of Decision-Making in Environmental
Conservation 155

Decision-Making in Philanthropic Grant Allocation 156

Applying Decision-Making in Sports Strategy. 157

Decision-Making in Digital Transformation 158

The Role of Decision-Making in Personal Development. 159

Leveraging Decision-Making in Project Evaluation and
Review 160

Decision-Making in Social Media Management. 161

Applying Decision-Making in Personal Conflict Resolution 162

Decision-Making in Product Development 163

The Role of Decision-Making in Talent Acquisition and
Management 164

Leveraging Decision-Making in Ethical Investing 165

Decision-Making in Virtual and Remote Work Environments . . .166

Applying Decision-Making in Competitive Analysis. 167

Decision-Making in Corporate Governance 168

The Role of Decision-Making in Personal Well-Being 169

Leveraging Decision-Making in Crisis Communication. 170

Decision-Making in Design Thinking 171

Applying Decision-Making in Data Privacy and Security 172

Decision-Making in Digital Marketing Strategy. 173

The Role of Decision-Making in Emotional Intelligence 174

Leveraging Decision-Making in Green and Sustainable
    Business Practices. 175

Decision-Making in Agile Project Management. 176

Applying Decision-Making in Crisis Leadership 177

Decision-Making in Diversity, Equity, and Inclusion 178

The Role of Decision-Making in Social Entrepreneurship. 179

Leveraging Decision-Making in Crisis Recovery 180

Decision-Making in Global Market Expansion. 181

Applying Decision-Making in Humanitarian Aid and
    Relief Efforts 182

Decision-Making in Personal Financial Planning. 183

The Role of Decision-Making in Digital Ethics 184

Leveraging Decision-Making in Public Transportation
    Planning. 185

Decision-Making in Personal Goal Setting 186

Applying Decision-Making in Philanthropic Collaboration 187

Decision-Making in Political Campaign Strategy. 188

The Role of Decision-Making in Sustainable Urban
    Planning. 189

Leveraging Decision-Making in Digital Transformation 190

Decision-Making in Public Safety and Emergency
    Management 191

Applying Decision-Making in Intellectual Property
    Management 192

Decision-Making in Crisis Prevention 193

The Role of Decision-Making in Community Development 194

Leveraging Decision-Making in Remote Learning and
    Education 195

Decision-Making in Cybersecurity Risk Management 196

Applying Decision-Making in Social Media Governance 197

Decision-Making in Disaster Resilience Planning 198

The Role of Decision-Making in Sustainable Tourism 199

Leveraging Decision-Making in Customer Experience
    Management 200

Decision-Making in Disaster Risk Reduction. 201

Applying Decision-Making in Mental Health Support. 202

Decision-Making in International Development Aid. 203

The Role of Decision-Making in Technology Ethics 204

Leveraging Decision-Making in Corporate Culture
    Transformation. 205

Decision-Making in Personal Conflict Resolution. 206

Applying Decision-Making in Sustainable Fashion. 207

Decision-Making in Workplace Diversity and Inclusion. 208

The Role of Decision-Making in Personal Growth and
    Development 209

Leveraging Decision-Making in Social Entrepreneurship. 210

Decision-Making in Crisis Resource Allocation 211

Applying Decision-Making in Health Policy 212

Decision-Making in Cross-Cultural Communication. 213

The Role of Decision-Making in Sustainable Agriculture 214

Leveraging Decision-Making in Digital Accessibility 215

Decision-Making in Innovation Ecosystems 216

Applying Decision-Making in Environmental Education 217

Decision-Making in Remote Team Management 218

The Role of Decision-Making in Ethical Leadership 219

Leveraging Decision-Making in Renewable Energy
    Transition 220

Decision-Making in Ethical Supply Chain Management 221

Applying Decision-Making in Urban Mobility Planning 222

Decision-Making in Personal Time Management. 223

The Role of Decision-Making in Green Building Design 224

Leveraging Decision-Making in International Trade and
    Globalization. 225

Decision-Making in Personal Financial Investments. 226

Applying Decision-Making in Healthcare Innovation 227

Decision-Making in Circular Economy Transition 228

The Role of Decision-Making in Interpersonal Relationships . . .229

Leveraging Decision-Making in Social Impact Investing 230

Decision-Making in Cybersecurity Governance. 231

Applying Decision-Making in Disaster Recovery and
    Reconstruction. 232

Decision-Making in Personal Health and Wellness. 233

The Role of Decision-Making in Innovation Leadership. 234

Leveraging Decision-Making in Environmental Impact
    Assessment. 235

Decision-Making in Team Diversity and Inclusion 236

Applying Decision-Making in Crisis Communication and
    Reputation Management 237

Decision-Making in Sustainable Tourism Development. 238

The Role of Decision-Making in Personal Relationship
    Building 239

Leveraging Decision-Making in Agile Leadership 240

Decision-Making in Crisis Mental Health Support 241

Applying Decision-Making in Human Rights Advocacy 242

Decision-Making in Personal Skill Development 243

The Role of Decision-Making in Social Media Influencing 244

Leveraging Decision-Making in Project Portfolio
    Management. 245

Decision-Making in Community Engagement and
Empowerment 246

Applying Decision-Making in Nonprofit Governance 247

Decision-Making in Digital Transformation Governance 248

The Role of Decision-Making in Sustainable Development
Planning. 249

Leveraging Decision-Making in Ethical AI Development. 250

Decision-Making in Disaster Preparedness Planning 251

Applying Decision-Making in Public Health Emergency
Response 252

Decision-Making in Personal Leadership Development. 253

The Role of Decision-Making in Sustainable Business
Practices. 254

Leveraging Decision-Making in Financial Risk Management . . .255

Decision-Making in Public Policy Formulation 256

Applying Decision-Making in Ethical Journalism 257

Decision-Making in Conflict Resolution and Mediation. 258

The Role of Decision-Making in Personal Well-being and
Work-Life Balance. 259

Leveraging Decision-Making in Social Innovation 260

Decision-Making in Data Privacy and Protection 261

Applying Decision-Making in Ethical Consumerism. 262

Decision-Making in Cultural Heritage Preservation 263

The Role of Decision-Making in Resilient Leadership 264

Leveraging Decision-Making in Community-Based
Disaster Risk Management 265

Decision-Making in Personal Ethical Dilemmas. 266

Applying Decision-Making in Entrepreneurial Ventures 267

Decision-Making in Sustainable Waste Management 268

The Role of Decision-Making in Conflict Transformation. 269

Leveraging Decision-Making in Digital Marketing
Strategies 270

Decision-Making in Sustainable Forest Management 271

Applying Decision-Making in Gender Equality Initiatives 272

Decision-Making in Workplace Safety and Health 273

The Role of Decision-Making in Global Climate Change
Mitigation. 274

Leveraging Decision-Making in Social Impact Measurement . . . 275

Decision-Making in Personal Goal Setting and Achievement . . . 276

Applying Decision-Making in Digital Privacy Education 277

Decision-Making in Sustainable Water Resource
Management 278

The Role of Decision-Making in Resilient Urban Planning 279

Leveraging Decision-Making in Corporate Social
Responsibility 280

Decision-Making in Sustainable Fashion and Apparel
Industry 281

Applying Decision-Making in Mental Health Advocacy. 282

Decision-Making in Sustainable Tourism Destination
Management 283

The Role of Decision-Making in Artificial Intelligence
Governance. 284

Leveraging Decision-Making in Philanthropic Investments 285

Decision-Making in Personal Conflict Resolution. 286

Applying Decision-Making in Energy Transition Planning. 287

Decision-Making in Corporate Governance and Ethics 288

The Role of Decision-Making in Social Justice Advocacy. 289

Leveraging Decision-Making in Sustainable Agriculture 290

Decision-Making in Ethical Leadership 291

Applying Decision-Making in Disaster Risk Reduction 292

Decision-Making in Accessible Technology Design 293

The Role of Decision-Making in Community Empowerment. . . . 294

Leveraging Decision-Making in Ethical Supply Chain
Management 295

Decision-Making in Personal Financial Planning 296

Applying Decision-Making in Public Art and Cultural
    Initiatives 297

Decision-Making in Sustainable Transportation Planning 298

The Role of Decision-Making in Personal Growth and
    Development 299

Leveraging Decision-Making in Digital Citizenship 300

Decision-Making in Sustainable Packaging Solutions 301

Conclusion 302

Introduction

Decisions shape our lives, defining the path we take and the outcomes we achieve. In this book, we will explore the immense power of decision-making and its impact on our personal growth and success.

The Man and His Car

Imagine a man who was fed up with his old, embarrassing car. Instead of accepting its mediocrity, he took a bold step. Armed with a shotgun, he shattered every window, destroyed every tire, and fired one hundred rounds into it. He had reached his breaking point. Surprisingly, instead of discarding it, he chose to save it. Later, when asked about his success, he proudly displayed his transformed car. It became a symbol of his determination and the power of his decision.

The Life-Changing
Nature of Decision Making

Every decision we make has the potential to be life changing. Imagine returning home today and dedicating the next few days to clearing up a list of decisions. This simple act could ignite inspiration for the next five or ten years. The day we can bring ourselves to decide is truly inspiring and transformative.

The Power of Desire

Desire is a mysterious force that compels us to pursue our dreams relentlessly. Sometimes, desire waits for a trigger, an event or experience that propels us forward. It could be a song, a movie, a seminar, or a conversation with a friend. We never know what will awaken our deepest desires, but when it happens, it holds immeasurable value.

Welcoming All Experiences

To unlock our potential, we must be open to all experiences. Often, we build walls to shield ourselves from disappointment, but in doing so, we also block out happiness. It is crucial to take down these walls and embrace every experience that comes our way. Each experience has the potential to teach us valuable lessons and shape our journey towards success.

The Power of Resolve

Resolve, characterized by the words "I will," is one of the most potent forces in the human language. It represents a promise we make to ourselves, a commitment to never give up. A wise young girl once defined resolve as promising oneself to never give up. This unwavering determination is the key to overcoming challenges and achieving our goals.

Persistence
in Learning to Walk

Consider a baby's journey to learn how to walk. No mother would ever give up on her baby's attempts to walk. The magic word here is "until." Promise yourself to keep going until you succeed. Apply this principle to your own life - read books until your skills improve, attend seminars until you gain a grasp of the subject, and practice relentlessly until you master the necessary skills. Never give up until you reach your desired outcome.

Discovering
Life's Treasures

By paying the price of persistence and unwavering resolve, we uncover some of life's most valuable treasures. The journey might be challenging, but the rewards are immeasurable. When we are willing to go the extra mile, push through obstacles, and refuse to give up, we open ourselves up to endless possibilities and a life full of fulfillment.

The Importance of
Clarity in Decision Making

Clarity is a vital aspect of effective decision-making. When we are clear about our goals, values, and priorities, it becomes easier to make decisions aligned with our desired outcomes. Take the time to reflect on what truly matters to you and set clear intentions for your future.

Embracing
Responsibility for Decisions

Decisions come with responsibility. Each choice we make shapes our reality and has consequences, both positive and negative. Embracing responsibility for our decisions empowers us to take ownership of our lives and create the outcomes we desire.

The Power of
Small Decisions

While some decisions have significant impacts, it is crucial not to overlook the power of small decisions. The choices we make in our everyday lives accumulate and shape our overall trajectory. Pay attention to the seemingly insignificant decisions and make choices that align with your long-term vision.

Overcoming
Decision Paralysis

Decision paralysis is a common obstacle that many people face. The fear of making the wrong choice can leave us stuck, unable to move forward. To overcome decision paralysis, break down complex decisions into smaller, manageable steps. Trust yourself and remember that acting, even if it leads to a mistake, is better than being paralyzed by indecision.

Making
Decisions Based on Values

Our values serve as a compass for decision-making. When faced with difficult choices, aligning them with our core values can provide clarity and a sense of purpose. Take the time to identify your values and use them as a guide to make decisions that resonate with who you truly are.

The Power of Intuition

Intuition, often referred to as a gut feeling, can be a valuable tool in decision-making. While it may not always be logical, our intuition taps into a deeper wisdom that can guide us towards the right path. Learn to trust your intuition and allow it to inform your decision-making process.

Seeking Wise Counsel

Sometimes, decisions can be overwhelming, and we may benefit from seeking advice from others. Surround yourself with trusted mentors, friends, or professionals who can provide valuable insights and perspectives. Remember, however, that the final decision rests with you, and it is essential to trust your own judgment.

Embracing
Failure as a Learning Opportunity

Not all decisions lead to the desired outcome, and that is okay. Failure is an inevitable part of life, but it is also a valuable teacher. Embrace failures as opportunities for growth and learning. Analyze what went wrong, extract lessons from the experience, and use that knowledge to make better decisions in the future.

The Art of
Decision Refinement

Decisions are not set in stone. As we gain new insights and experiences, it is essential to refine our decisions accordingly. Be open to adjusting your course, making changes when necessary, and staying adaptable in the face of evolving circumstances.

The Ripple Effect of Decisions

Decisions have a ripple effect, impacting not only our own lives but also the lives of those around us. Consider the potential consequences of your choices on others and strive to make decisions that promote harmony, empathy, and positive growth for all involved.

Cultivating Patience and Trust
in the Decision-Making Process

Good decisions often require patience and trust. Avoid rushing into choices out of desperation or impatience. Take the time to gather information, weigh the pros and cons, and trust that the right decision will reveal itself in due time.

The Impact of
Fear on Decision Making

Fear often holds us back from making bold and transformative decisions. It whispers doubts and insecurities into our minds, making us question our abilities and the potential outcomes. Recognize that fear is a natural part of the decision-making process but do not let it control you. Embrace fear as an opportunity for growth and use it as fuel to push past your comfort zone.

Setting Clear Goals and Objectives

Clarity in decision-making goes hand in hand with setting clear goals and objectives. Define what you want to achieve and create a roadmap to guide your decisions. Having a clear destination in mind helps you make choices that align with your long-term vision.

The Art of Prioritization

In a world filled with endless options and possibilities, learning to prioritize is crucial. Not every decision carries the same weight or urgency. Identify your priorities and focus your energy on the decisions that will have the greatest impact on your goals and aspirations.

Avoiding Decision Overload

Decision overload can be overwhelming and lead to analysis paralysis. When faced with numerous options, break them down into smaller, manageable groups. By narrowing your choices, you can make more informed decisions without feeling overwhelmed by the abundance of possibilities.

Developing
a Decision-Making Framework

Creating a decision-making framework can provide structure and clarity in the face of complex choices. Define your decision criteria, weigh the pros and cons, and consider the long-term consequences. This framework acts as a guiding tool, helping you make consistent and informed decisions.

Learning
from Past Decisions

Reflecting on past decisions can offer valuable insights for future choices. Analyze the outcomes of previous decisions and assess what worked and what did not. Use this knowledge to refine your decision-making process and make more informed choices moving forward.

Considering
the Short-Term and Long-Term Impact

Decisions can have both short-term and long-term consequences. While immediate gratification might be tempting, consider the long-term impact of your choices. Will it align with your values and contribute to your overall goals? Taking a holistic view ensures that your decisions have a positive impact on your life as a whole.

Embracing
Flexibility and Adaptability

In a rapidly changing world, being flexible and adaptable in decision-making is essential. Circumstances can shift, new information can arise, and unexpected challenges may appear. Embrace the ability to pivot and adjust your decisions when necessary to stay aligned with your goals.

The Power of Visualization

Visualization is a powerful tool that can enhance decision-making. Take the time to imagine the potential outcomes of your choices. Visualize the desired result and how it aligns with your goals. This mental exercise can provide clarity and confidence in making the right decision.

Trusting Your Instincts

While rational analysis is essential, do not discount the power of your instincts. Trust your gut feelings and intuition. Sometimes, our subconscious mind holds valuable insights that our conscious mind may overlook. Allow your intuition to guide you in making decisions that resonate deep within you.

The Role of
Emotions in Decision Making

Emotions play a significant role in decision-making, often influencing our choices more than we realize. It is important to be aware of your emotional state when making decisions. Take the time to understand and manage your emotions, ensuring they align with your values and long-term goals.

Seeking
Diverse Perspectives

To make well-rounded decisions, it is essential to seek diverse perspectives. Surround yourself with individuals who have different backgrounds, experiences, and opinions. This diversity of thought can offer valuable insights and challenge your assumptions, leading to more informed and thoughtful decisions.

The Balance
between Logic and Intuition

Decision-making is a delicate balance between logic and intuition. While logic provides a rational framework, intuition taps into our subconscious wisdom. Cultivate the ability to integrate both aspects, utilizing logical analysis while also trusting your intuition when appropriate.

The Power of
Reflective Thinking

In the fast-paced world we live in, taking the time for reflective thinking is often overlooked. Set aside dedicated moments to reflect on your decisions and their outcomes. What lessons can be learned? How can you improve your decision-making process? Reflective thinking allows for continuous growth and refinement.

Harnessing
the Power of Information

Information is a valuable resource when making decisions. Seek out reliable sources of information, gather relevant data, and conduct thorough research. Well-informed decisions have a higher likelihood of success and positive outcomes.

The Art of Compromise

Not all decisions involve clear-cut choices. Sometimes, compromise is necessary to find a middle ground that satisfies multiple stakeholders. Be open to considering alternative perspectives and finding solutions that balance various interests.

Embracing
Uncertainty and Risk

Decision-making often involves an element of uncertainty and risk. Embrace the unknown and be willing to take calculated risks when necessary. Recognize that not every decision will guarantee success, but the lessons learned from taking risks can lead to invaluable growth and opportunity.

The Impact of
Decision Making on Others

Our decisions can have a profound impact on the lives of others. Consider the potential consequences and implications for those affected by your choices. Act with empathy, compassion, and a sense of responsibility towards others when making decisions.

Learning
to Let Go of Regret

Regret can hinder our ability to make future decisions confidently. Accept that mistakes and regrets are part of the human experience. Learn from them. But do not let them hold you back. Embrace a mindset of growth and use past experiences as steppingstones toward better decision-making.

The Power of
Decision-Making Skills

Decision-making is a skill. You can be developed and honed over time. Embrace opportunities to learn and practice decision-making in various contexts. As you strengthen your decision-making skills, you will gain confidence and make more effective choices.

Cultivating
a Growth Mindset in Decision Making

A growth mindset is essential for effective decision-making. Embrace the belief. Your abilities and intelligence can be developed. All it needs is your dedication and hard work. This mindset allows you to approach decisions with a willingness to learn from mistakes and adapt your strategies.

Avoiding
Analysis Paralysis

Analysis paralysis occurs when we become overwhelmed by excessive information and options, hindering our ability to make decisions. To overcome this, set clear decision-making parameters, limit your information gathering to what is necessary, and establish a deadline for making a choice. Trust your instincts and have confidence in your ability to make a thoughtful decision.

Understanding
the Power of Timing

Timing can significantly impact the success of a decision. Some decisions require immediate action, while others benefit from careful timing and patience. Assess the urgency and consider whether delaying a decision may provide additional clarity or options.

Balancing Short-Term Gratification with Long-Term Goals

In the face of temptation for instant gratification, it is important to weigh short-term desires against long-term goals. Ask yourself if a decision aligns with your overarching objectives. By making choices that prioritize long-term growth and fulfillment, you position yourself for sustainable success.

Learning
from Successful Decision-Makers

Study the decision-making processes of successful individuals and leaders. Read biographies, listen to interviews, and seek out mentors who can offer guidance and share their experiences. Learning from those who have achieved success through effective decision-making can provide valuable insights and inspiration.

Applying
Critical Thinking Skills

Critical thinking involves objectively analyzing information, questioning assumptions, and evaluating alternative perspectives. Develop your critical thinking skills to make well-reasoned decisions. Practice discerning between facts and opinions and seek evidence to support your choices.

Setting
Realistic Expectations

When making decisions, it is essential to set realistic expectations. Avoid falling into the trap of overly optimistic or pessimistic thinking. Consider both best-case and worst-case scenarios and develop contingency plans to mitigate risks and challenges.

The Power of Incremental Progress

Not all decisions need to result in immediate, drastic changes. Embrace the power of incremental progress by making small, consistent decisions that move you closer to your goals. Each small step contributes to significant growth over time.

Seeking
Continuous Feedback

Feedback is a valuable tool for improving decision-making skills. Seek feedback from trusted mentors, colleagues, or friends who can provide constructive insights and help you identify blind spots. Use feedback as an opportunity for growth and refinement.

Embracing
Decision-Making as a Journey

Decision-making is an ongoing journey rather than a one-time event. Embrace the process, knowing that each decision you make contributes to your personal and professional development. Embrace both successes and failures as opportunities for growth and learning.

Emphasizing
Ethical Decision Making

Ethics should be at the forefront of our decision-making process. Consider the moral implications and potential impact on others when making choices. Strive to align your decisions with principles of honesty, integrity, and fairness, ensuring that your actions uphold ethical standards.

Evaluating
the Long-Term Consequences

When making decisions, it is important to look beyond immediate outcomes and consider the long-term consequences. Assess how your choices may impact your future, relationships, and overall well-being. Making decisions with a long-term perspective can lead to more sustainable and fulfilling outcomes.

Cultivating
Emotional Intelligence

Emotional intelligence plays a crucial role in decision-making. Develop your self-awareness, empathy, and emotional management skills. By understanding and acknowledging your emotions, you can make decisions that are more balanced and aligned with your values.

Harnessing
the Power of Data and Analytics

In today's data-driven world, leveraging data and analytics can enhance decision-making. Utilize available data to gain insights, identify patterns, and inform your choices. Combine quantitative analysis with your intuition to make well-informed decisions.

Avoiding
Decision Fatigue

Constant decision-making can lead to decision fatigue, causing a decline in the quality of choices. Recognize when you are mentally exhausted and take breaks or delegate decisions when possible. By managing decision fatigue, you can maintain clarity and make better choices.

Promoting
Collaboration in Decision Making

Collaboration brings diverse perspectives together and fosters more robust decision-making. Seek input from others, encourage brainstorming, and foster a collaborative environment. By involving stakeholders in the decision-making process, you can benefit from collective wisdom and achieve better outcomes.

Embracing
Innovation and Creativity

Innovation and creativity can transform decision-making. Embrace new ideas, explore unconventional solutions, and challenge traditional thinking. Foster an environment that encourages innovation, and do not be afraid to take calculated risks in pursuit of novel and impactful decisions.

The Importance of Self-Reflection

Regular self-reflection is crucial for personal growth and improved decision-making. Set aside time to reflect on past decisions, assess their outcomes, and identify areas for improvement. Self-reflection enhances self-awareness and empowers you to make more intentional and effective choices.

Recognizing
the Power of Adaptation

The ability to adapt and pivot in decision-making is essential in a rapidly changing world. Be open to adjusting your decisions when new information emerges, or circumstances evolve. Embrace flexibility and agility to navigate the complexities of decision-making successfully.

The Role of
Accountability in Decision Making

Accountability is integral to decision-making. Take responsibility for your choices and their consequences. Learn from both successes and failures and use these experiences to improve future decision-making. Holding yourself accountable fosters growth, learning, and a sense of ownership in your decisions.

Fostering
a Culture of Decision-Making

Decision-making is not solely an individual endeavor but also a collective responsibility. Foster a culture within your organization or community that values and encourages thoughtful decision-making. Create spaces for open dialogue, collaboration, and the sharing of diverse perspectives.

The Role of
Intention in Decision Making

Intentionality shapes the quality of our decisions. Clarify your intentions and align them with your values and goals. When your intentions are clear, the decisions you make will be more purposeful and impactful.

Developing
Decision-Making Resilience

Resilience is key when faced with the challenges and uncertainties of decision-making. Learn to bounce back from setbacks and adapt to unexpected outcomes. Cultivate a resilient mindset that sees failures as learning opportunities and keeps you motivated to persist in decision-making.

Embracing
Decision-Making as a Learning Journey

View decision-making as an ongoing learning journey rather than a series of isolated choices. Each decision provides an opportunity to learn more about yourself, others, and the world around you. Embrace the lessons embedded in the decision-making process to continually grow and evolve.

Applying
Ethical Decision-Making Frameworks

Ethical decision-making frameworks provide a structured approach to navigating complex moral dilemmas. Familiarize yourself with established frameworks such as consequentialism, deontology, and virtue ethics. Use these frameworks to analyze ethical considerations and make principled decisions.

Balancing
Rationality and Intuition

Decision-making involves a delicate balance between rationality and intuition. While rational analysis is valuable, do not discount the wisdom of intuition. Cultivate a harmonious relationship between these two faculties, allowing each to inform and complement the other in decision-making.

Leveraging
Technology in Decision-Making

Technology offers powerful tools to enhance decision-making processes. Utilize data analytics, artificial intelligence, and decision-support systems to gather insights, streamline information, and improve the accuracy of your choices. However, remain mindful of the ethical implications and biases that can arise with technology.

Reflecting
on Systemic and Societal Implications

Expand your perspective beyond individual decisions and consider their broader systemic and societal implications. Reflect on how your choices may impact marginalized communities, the environment, or broader social issues. Strive to make decisions that contribute to a more just and sustainable world.

Balancing
Confidence and Humility

Confidence is important in decision-making, but it must be balanced with humility. Acknowledge that you do not have all the answers. Be open to learning from others. Embrace a growth mindset that allows for continuous improvement and seeks feedback to refine your decision-making abilities.

Celebrating
Decision-Making Successes

Celebrate your decision-making successes, both big and small. Acknowledge and appreciate the positive outcomes that result from thoughtful choices. Celebrating these successes reinforces your confidence and motivates you to continue making effective decisions.

Navigating
Ethical Dilemmas

Ethical dilemmas can be challenging to navigate, requiring careful consideration of competing values and moral principles. Develop strategies for effectively resolving ethical conflicts, such as seeking guidance from trusted advisors, conducting thorough research, and reflecting on the potential consequences of each possible choice.

Leveraging
Emotional Intelligence in Decision Making

Emotional intelligence plays a significant role in decision-making, as it helps us understand and manage our own emotions and empathize with others. Cultivate emotional intelligence by practicing self-awareness, active listening, and empathy. This will enable you to make decisions that consider both rationality and the emotional well-being of those involved.

Recognizing
Bias in Decision Making

Human beings are prone to biases that can influence decision making. Familiarize yourself with common cognitive biases such as confirmation bias, availability bias, and anchoring bias. By recognizing and addressing these biases, you can make more objective and unbiased decisions.

Embracing
Diversity and Inclusion in Decision Making

Diverse perspectives contribute to well-rounded decision-making. Embrace diversity and inclusion by actively seeking out and valuing different viewpoints, backgrounds, and experiences. This fosters a more comprehensive understanding of complex issues and leads to more robust and inclusive decisions.

Evaluating
the Costs and Benefits of Decisions

Every decision comes with costs and benefits. Conduct a thorough analysis of the potential risks and rewards associated with each choice. Consider the short-term and long-term implications, financial aspects, and impact on stakeholders. By evaluating the costs and benefits, you can make informed decisions that maximize positive outcomes.

Developing
Decision-Making Rituals

Establishing rituals or routines around decision-making can help streamline the process and enhance your focus and clarity. This could include practices such as journaling, meditation, or seeking solitude to reflect. Find rituals that work for you and incorporate them into your decision-making practice.

Leveraging
Decision-Making Tools and Models

Numerous decision-making tools and models exist to support the process. Some popular examples include the SWOT analysis, decision trees, and the Pareto principle. Familiarize yourself with these tools and models to assist in structuring your decision-making approach.

Practicing
Mindfulness in Decision Making

Mindfulness cultivates present-moment awareness and helps reduce distractions and impulsive decision-making. Practice mindfulness techniques such as deep breathing, meditation, or body scanning before making important decisions. This will help you approach choices with a calm and focused mindset.

Mitigating
Decision-Making Biases

Biases can hinder our ability to make objective decisions. Take steps to mitigate biases by seeking diverse perspectives, challenging assumptions, and engaging in critical thinking. Encourage others to challenge your decisions and provide alternative viewpoints to counteract bias.

Striving for Ethical Leadership
in Decision Making

As a leader, your decision-making carries significant weight and influences those around you. Strive to be an ethical leader by modeling integrity, transparency, and accountability in your decisions. Consider the long-term impact on your team, organization, and society as you make choices that align with ethical principles.

Harnessing
the Power of Intentional Decision-Making

Intentional decision-making involves aligning your choices with your core values, goals, and aspirations. Cultivate mindfulness and clarity to ensure that each decision is made with a purpose and a deep understanding of its potential impact.

Applying
Decision-Making to Personal Relationships

Decision-making extends beyond professional contexts and can greatly influence our personal relationships. Whether it is communicating effectively, resolving conflicts, or making joint decisions with loved ones, applying sound decision-making principles can enhance the quality of our interactions and strengthen our relationships.

Balancing
Logic and Emotion in Decision Making

Effective decision-making requires a balance between rational analysis and emotional consideration. Acknowledge the role of emotions in decision-making and explore how they can complement or challenge logical reasoning. Strive for a harmonious integration of both aspects to make choices that align with your values and resonate with your emotions.

Embracing
Failure as a Steppingstone to Success

Failure is an inevitable part of the decision-making journey. Rather than fearing failure, embrace it. It is an opportunity for growth and learning. Analyze failures objectively, extract valuable lessons, and use them to refine your decision-making process. Every failure brings you one step closer to success.

Recognizing the Influence
of Social and Cultural Factors

Social and cultural factors significantly impact our decision-making processes. Be aware of how societal norms, expectations, and biases influence your choices. Challenge assumptions and broaden your perspective to make decisions that are inclusive, equitable, and considerate of diverse backgrounds and experiences.

Empowering
Others in Decision Making

Decision-making should not be limited to individuals in positions of authority. Empower others by involving them in the decision-making process. Foster a collaborative environment where everyone's voice is heard and valued. This inclusivity enhances creativity, generates a sense of ownership, and leads to more robust and effective decisions.

Building Resilience
in the Face of Decision-Making Challenges

Decision-making can be accompanied by uncertainty, doubt, and fear of making the wrong choice. Build resilience by developing coping strategies, practicing self-care, and seeking support from trusted individuals. Cultivating resilience enables you to navigate decision-making challenges with greater confidence and adaptability.

Emphasizing
Sustainable Decision Making

Sustainability should be a guiding principle in decision-making. Consider the long-term environmental, social, and economic impact of your choices. Strive to make decisions that support ecological balance, social justice, and economic viability. By prioritizing sustainability, you contribute to a healthier and more equitable future.

Engaging
in Continuous Learning and Growth

Decision-making is a skill that can be refined through continuous learning and personal growth. Stay curious, seek knowledge, and embrace new experiences. Reflect on past decisions, evaluate their outcomes, and integrate the lessons learned into your decision-making approach.

Celebrating
Decision-Making Independence

As you gain confidence and expertise in decision-making, celebrate your ability to make independent choices. Trust your judgment and value your autonomy. Embrace the freedom and responsibility that comes with decision-making and use it as a catalyst for personal and professional growth.

Balancing
Short-Term and Long-Term Considerations

Effective decision-making requires balancing short-term and long-term considerations. While immediate outcomes may be tempting, it is essential to weigh the potential long-term impact of your choices. Strive for decisions that align with your long-term goals, values, and overall well-being.

Adapting
to Changing Circumstances

Decision-making is not a static process but one that requires adaptability. Circumstances may change, new information may emerge, or unexpected events may occur. Stay flexible and be willing to adjust your decisions when necessary. Embrace a mindset that embraces change and allows for continuous adaptation.

Recognizing
and Mitigating Decision-Making Biases

Decision-making biases can cloud our judgment and lead to suboptimal choices. Become familiar with common biases such as confirmation bias, anchoring bias, and hindsight bias. By recognizing and actively mitigating these biases, you can make more objective and informed decisions.

Cultivating
a Supportive Decision-Making Environment

Surround yourself with a supportive network that encourages and challenges your decision-making process. Seek out mentors, advisors, or peers who can offer guidance, diverse perspectives, and constructive feedback. Create an environment that fosters open dialogue and nurtures personal and professional growth.

Embracing
Intuition as a Valuable Guide

Intuition is a powerful tool in decision-making, often drawing upon unconscious knowledge and experiences. Trust your gut feelings and give intuition a seat at the table alongside logical analysis. Cultivate self-awareness to differentiate between intuition and impulsive reactions, harnessing wisdom for more holistic decision-making.

Learning from Others'
Decision-Making Experiences

Learn from the decision-making experiences of others, both successes and failures. Read case studies, listen to podcasts, or engage in conversations with individuals who have faced similar choices. Extract valuable insights and apply them to your own decision-making process.

Using
Visualization Techniques

Visualization is a powerful technique to enhance decision-making. Picture the potential outcomes of different choices, imagining how they align with your goals and values. Visualize the emotions and impact associated with each option, helping you make decisions that resonate deeply within you.

Evaluating
the Opportunity Cost

Every decision comes with an opportunity cost, the potential value or benefit sacrificed by choosing one option over another. Consider the trade-offs and weigh the benefits against the costs. Evaluate what you stand to gain and lose in different scenarios, helping you make more informed and strategic decisions.

Taking
Responsibility for Decision Outcomes

Taking responsibility for the outcomes of your decisions is crucial for personal and professional growth. Acknowledge the role you played in the decision-making process, whether the results are positive or negative. Learn from the outcomes, make necessary adjustments, and use them as steppingstones for future success.

Celebrating
the Decision-Making Journey

Decision-making is an ongoing journey filled with opportunities for growth, learning, and self-discovery. Celebrate your progress, milestones, and the insights gained along the way. Embrace the challenges and triumphs of decision-making, recognizing that each choice has the potential to shape your life in meaningful ways.

Leveraging
Decision-Making in Team Settings

Decision-making in team settings requires collaboration, communication, and consensus-building. Foster a culture of active participation and inclusivity, ensuring that all team members have a voice in the decision-making process. Encourage constructive debates and leverage the collective intelligence of the team to make well-informed choices.

Evaluating
Decision-Making Risks

Every decision carries inherent risks. Evaluate the potential risks associated with each choice and develop risk mitigation strategies. Consider factors such as financial risks, reputational risks, and the potential impact on stakeholders. By proactively addressing risks, you can make decisions with greater confidence and minimize negative outcomes.

Nurturing
Ethical Decision-Making in Organizations

Ethical decision-making is vital for maintaining trust, integrity, and ethical conduct within organizations. Foster a culture that values ethical behavior by establishing clear ethical guidelines, promoting transparency, and providing training on ethical decision-making. Encourage employees to uphold ethical standards and hold them accountable for their choices.

Embracing
Decision-Making as a Driver of Innovation

Decision-making is intricately linked to innovation. Encourage a mindset of experimentation and risk-taking, empowering individuals to make decisions that foster creativity and drive innovation. Embrace a culture that supports learning from failures, as innovation often stems from the willingness to explore new possibilities.

Leveraging
Decision-Making in Personal Growth

Personal growth is closely tied to decision-making. Embrace decisions as opportunities for self-discovery, self-improvement, and personal transformation. Reflect on how each choice aligns with your values, aspirations, and personal development goals. Use decision-making as a catalyst for continuous growth and self-fulfillment.

Fostering
Decision-Making Confidence

Building confidence in decision-making is essential for making assertive choices. Cultivate self-confidence by recognizing your strengths, acknowledging past successes, and learning from failures. Surround yourself with supportive individuals who believe in your decision-making abilities, further boosting your confidence.

Incorporating
Feedback Loops in Decision Making

Feedback loops provide valuable insights and facilitate continuous improvement in decision-making. Seek feedback from stakeholders affected by your choices and use it to refine your decision-making process. Regularly evaluate the outcomes of decisions, learn from them, and adjust your approach accordingly.

The Role of
Decision-Making in Crisis Management

Effective decision-making is critical during times of crisis. Develop crisis management protocols, establish decision-making frameworks, and identify key decision-makers in advance. Ensure that decisions are made swiftly, considering the immediate needs and long-term impact of crisis situations.

Balancing
Decisiveness and Analysis

Striking a balance between decisiveness and analysis is crucial in decision-making. Avoid rushing into decisions without adequate thought and analysis. However, also be mindful of analysis paralysis and the potential cost of delayed decision-making. Find the right balance by gathering necessary information while maintaining a sense of urgency.

Embracing
the Evolution of Decision-Making

Decision-making is a dynamic process that evolves over time. Embrace the ever-changing nature of decision-making by staying open to new approaches, strategies, and tools. Adapt to advancements in technology, evolving societal norms, and emerging research to continuously enhance your decision-making capabilities.

Utilizing
Decision-Making in Personal Finance

Sound decision-making is essential in personal finance. Develop a financial plan, set clear financial goals, and make informed choices regarding savings, investments, and expenses. Consider the potential long-term consequences of financial decisions and seek advice from financial experts when needed.

Embracing
Decision-Making in Health and Wellness

Decision-making plays a significant role in maintaining health and wellness. Make choices that prioritize exercise, nutrition, stress management, and self-care. Evaluate the potential risks and benefits of healthcare options and consult healthcare professionals for guidance in making informed decisions about your well-being.

The Impact of
Decision-Making on the Environment

Our decisions have a direct impact on the environment. Make environmentally conscious choices, such as reducing waste, conserving energy, and supporting sustainable practices. Educate yourself on the environmental implications of your decisions and seek ways to minimize your ecological footprint.

Cultivating
Decision-Making in Education

Decision-making is integral to education. Encourage students to develop critical thinking skills, consider different perspectives, and make informed choices. Teach decision-making as a lifelong skill, empowering students to navigate their educational journeys and make choices aligned with their academic and personal growth.

The Role of
Decision-Making in Entrepreneurship

Entrepreneurship requires effective decision-making at every stage. Evaluate market opportunities, assess risks, and make strategic choices to drive business growth. Embrace calculated risks, adapt to changing market conditions, and learn from both successes and failures to navigate the entrepreneurial landscape.

Applying
Decision-Making in Conflict Resolution

Decision-making is crucial in conflict resolution. Consider the needs and perspectives of all parties involved, seek common ground, and make choices that promote understanding and collaboration. Utilize effective communication and negotiation skills to find mutually beneficial solutions to conflicts.

Decision-Making in
Ethical Dilemmas in Medicine

Ethical dilemmas are common in medicine. Healthcare professionals must navigate complex choices that impact patients' lives. Apply ethical frameworks and principles to make decisions that prioritize patient well-being, autonomy, and justice. Consult colleagues and ethics committees when faced with challenging ethical situations.

Incorporating Decision-Making in
Social Justice Advocacy

Social justice advocacy often involves making decisions that address systemic inequalities and promote fairness. Consider the potential impact of advocacy choices on marginalized communities and work collaboratively to develop strategies that drive positive social change. Prioritize inclusivity, equity, and empowerment in decision-making processes.

The Role of Decision-Making in Personal Relationships

Decision-making heavily influences personal relationships. Make choices that promote open communication, respect, and mutual growth. Consider the needs and desires of others and engage in collaborative decision-making to ensure healthy and fulfilling relationships.

Cultivating
Decision-Making in Parenting

Parenting requires numerous decisions that shape a child's life. Embrace a thoughtful and values-driven approach to parenting decisions. Consider the child's well-being, individuality, and long-term development when making choices about education, discipline, and extracurricular activities.

Integrating
Decision-Making in Project Management

Effective project management relies on sound decision-making. Develop a systematic approach to decision-making within projects, considering factors such as project goals, timelines, resource allocation, and stakeholder needs. Utilize decision-making tools, risk assessment, and feedback loops to ensure successful project outcomes.

The Role of Decision-Making in Public Policy

Public policy decisions have far-reaching implications for society. Consider diverse perspectives, engage stakeholders, and conduct thorough research when making policy choices. Strive for evidence-based decision-making that addresses societal challenges, promotes equality, and fosters the well-being of all citizens.

Balancing
Personal and Professional Decision-Making

Balancing personal and professional decision-making is a constant challenge. Recognize that the choices you make in one domain can impact the other. Strive for alignment between your personal values and professional goals, making choices that integrate both spheres harmoniously.

Decision-Making in Philanthropy and Social Impact

Philanthropy and social impact initiatives require thoughtful decision-making. Assess the potential impact of philanthropic choices, conduct due diligence on organizations and causes, and engage in strategic philanthropy that maximizes positive social change. Evaluate the effectiveness and outcomes of your philanthropic efforts to continuously refine your decision-making in this realm.

The Role of Decision-Making in Crisis Communication

During times of crisis, decision-making in communication is vital. Make timely and informed decisions about communication strategies, messaging, and stakeholder engagement. Consider the potential reputational impact, transparency, and empathy when making decisions to effectively manage crisis situations.

Applying Decision-Making in Technology Development

Technology development relies on effective decision-making to drive innovation and progress. Evaluate technological options, anticipate potential risks and benefits, and make informed choices about research and development. Incorporate ethical considerations, user feedback, and market demands into decision-making processes.

Decision-Making in
Legal and Ethical Dilemmas

Legal and ethical dilemmas require careful decision-making to uphold justice and fairness. Apply legal frameworks, consider ethical principles, consult legal experts, and engage in thorough analysis to make decisions that align with legal and moral obligations.

Incorporating Decision-Making in Supply Chain Management

Effective supply chain management relies on sound decision-making. Evaluate suppliers, consider cost-efficiency, assess risks, and make choices that optimize logistics and operations. Incorporate sustainability and social responsibility considerations into supply chain decision-making for a more responsible and resilient system.

Decision-Making in
Mergers and Acquisitions

Mergers and acquisitions involve complex decisions that impact organizations and stakeholders. Evaluate financial implications, strategic alignment, cultural fit, and potential risks when making decisions about mergers and acquisitions. Engage in thorough due diligence and seek expert advice to ensure successful integration and growth.

Cultivating Decision-Making in Scientific Research

Scientific research requires careful decision-making to drive knowledge advancement. Design experiments, analyze data, and make choices that adhere to scientific principles and ethical standards. Foster a culture of rigorous and transparent decision-making to enhance the integrity and impact of scientific research.

Decision-Making in
Human Resources Management

Human resources management involves critical decision-making related to recruitment, performance evaluation, training, and employee well-being. Consider organizational goals, legal requirements, and employee needs when making HR decisions. Foster a supportive and inclusive work environment that values employee input in decision-making processes.

Applying Decision-Making in
Risk Management

Risk management requires effective decision-making to identify, assess, and mitigate potential risks. Evaluate the probability and impact of risks, develop risk management strategies, and make choices that minimize vulnerabilities. Regularly review and update risk management plans to adapt to changing circumstances.

Decision-Making in
Project Prioritization

When faced with multiple projects, prioritization is crucial. Evaluate the strategic alignment, resource availability, and potential impact of each project. Make informed choices about project sequencing and resource allocation to maximize overall organizational success.

Decision-Making in
Sales and Marketing

Sales and marketing decisions significantly impact business success. Analyze market trends, consumer behavior, and competitive landscapes to make choices that optimize sales and marketing strategies. Consider pricing, promotion, distribution, and product development when making decisions in these areas.

The Role of Decision-Making in Personal Productivity

Personal productivity relies on effective decision-making. Prioritize tasks, allocate time and resources wisely, and make choices that align with your goals and values. Practice self-discipline and self-awareness to enhance your decision-making process and maximize your productivity.

Decision-Making in
Quality Management

Quality management requires systematic decision-making to ensure product and service excellence. Establish quality standards, monitor performance, and make choices that improve processes and customer satisfaction. Use data-driven insights and customer feedback to continuously enhance quality management practices.

Applying Decision-Making in International Business

International business decisions require an understanding of cultural, political, and economic factors. Evaluate market entry strategies, assess risks and opportunities, and make choices that align with global business objectives. Consider cross-cultural communication, legal requirements, and market adaptation when expanding internationally.

Decision-Making in
Nonprofit Organizations

Decision-making in nonprofit organizations is unique due to the social impact focus. Consider the organization's mission, community needs, and stakeholder interests when making decisions. Balance financial sustainability with the organization's social goals to ensure long-term effectiveness and impact.

The Role of Decision-Making in Government Policies

Government policies have far-reaching implications for societies and nations. Evaluate social, economic, and environmental factors when making policy decisions. Engage stakeholders, consider expert advice, and assess potential consequences to develop policies that promote public welfare and long-term sustainability.

Decision-Making in
Personal Time Management

Personal time management relies on effective decision-making to allocate time to various activities and responsibilities. Set clear priorities, establish boundaries, and make choices that align with your values and personal goals. Regularly evaluate and adjust your time management strategies to maintain a healthy work-life balance.

Leveraging Decision-Making in
Supply Chain Optimization

Optimizing supply chains requires strategic decision-making. Evaluate factors such as demand forecasting, inventory management, transportation logistics, and supplier relationships. Make informed choices that streamline operations, reduce costs, and enhance customer satisfaction throughout the supply chain.

Decision-Making in Organizational Change Management

Organizational change management involves making decisions that navigate transitions effectively. Evaluate the need for change, develop change management plans, and make choices that facilitate smooth transitions and minimize resistance. Communicate transparently and engage employees in decision-making to foster buy-in and successful change implementation.

Applying Decision-Making in
Crisis Response

Crisis response requires swift and decisive decision-making. Assess the situation, gather relevant information, and make choices that prioritize the safety and well-being of individuals affected by the crisis. Communicate effectively and collaborate with stakeholders to coordinate crisis response efforts.

Decision-Making in
Customer Service Excellence

Delivering exceptional customer service requires effective decision-making. Empower customer service representatives to make choices that prioritize customer satisfaction, resolve issues, and exceed expectations. Develop guidelines and training programs that enable employees to make informed and customer-centric decisions.

The Role of Decision-Making in Innovation Management

Innovation management relies on strategic decision-making to drive creativity and breakthroughs. Evaluate ideas, prioritize innovation projects, and make choices that foster a culture of innovation. Encourage experimentation, embrace calculated risks, and leverage customer insights to fuel innovation within the organization.

Decision-Making in Corporate Social Responsibility

Corporate social responsibility (CSR) decisions have a significant impact on an organization's reputation and societal contribution. Make choices that align with CSR values, address environmental and social issues, and promote sustainable practices. Engage stakeholders, measure impacts, and continuously improve CSR initiatives through informed decision-making.

Leveraging Decision-Making in Financial Risk Management

Financial risk management requires sound decision-making to identify, assess, and mitigate financial risks. Evaluate market conditions, assess risk exposure, and make choices that optimize risk-reward trade-offs. Develop risk management strategies that safeguard financial stability and protect against potential losses.

Decision-Making in
Public Relations and Reputation Management

Public relations and reputation management decisions influence how organizations are perceived by the public. Evaluate messaging, media relations, and crisis communication strategies when making decisions in this domain. Actively manage and protect the organization's reputation through transparent and ethical decision-making practices.

Applying Decision-Making in Knowledge Management

Knowledge management involves making choices to capture, organize, and leverage organizational knowledge. Assess knowledge needs, develop knowledge-sharing strategies, and make decisions that enhance collaboration and knowledge flow. Foster a culture that values continuous learning and innovation through effective decision-making in knowledge management.

The Role of Decision-Making in Business Ethics

Business ethics decisions impact an organization's integrity, reputation, and long-term success. Evaluate ethical dilemmas, consider legal and moral obligations, and make choices that prioritize ethical conduct and stakeholder well-being. Foster an ethical culture through transparent decision-making and accountability.

Decision-Making in Cultural Sensitivity

Cultural sensitivity is essential in decision-making to respect diverse cultural norms and values. Consider cultural differences, historical contexts, and social dynamics when making choices that impact individuals from different cultures. Embrace cultural humility and actively seek input from diverse perspectives to ensure inclusive and culturally sensitive decision-making.

Leveraging Decision-Making in Data Analytics

Data analytics plays a crucial role in decision-making across various industries. Analyze data, extract meaningful insights, and make choices based on data-driven evidence. Utilize data visualization tools and statistical techniques to enhance the accuracy and effectiveness of decision-making in data-driven environments.

Decision-Making in
Public Health Management

Public health management requires informed decision-making to protect and promote population health. Assess epidemiological data, evaluate intervention strategies, and make choices that prioritize public health outcomes. Collaborate with healthcare professionals, policymakers, and community members to make evidence-based decisions in public health management.

Applying Decision-Making in
Disaster Preparedness and Response

Disaster preparedness and response decisions are critical in mitigating the impact of emergencies. Evaluate potential risks, develop emergency plans, and make choices that prioritize the safety and well-being of individuals and communities. Coordinate with relevant stakeholders and communicate effectively to ensure efficient and effective disaster response.

Decision-Making in
Artificial Intelligence and Machine Learning

Artificial intelligence (AI) and machine learning (ML) decisions have a profound impact on technology development and automation. Assess the ethical implications, potential biases, and privacy considerations associated with AI and ML systems. Make choices that prioritize fairness, transparency, and human well-being in the development and deployment of AI and ML technologies.

The Role of Decision-Making in Environmental Conservation

Environmental conservation decisions are vital for protecting natural resources and ecosystems. Evaluate the ecological impact of choices, consider sustainability principles, and make decisions that promote biodiversity, reduce pollution, and mitigate climate change. Advocate for environmental policies and engage in sustainable practices to support conservation efforts.

Decision-Making in Philanthropic Grant Allocation

Philanthropic grant allocation decisions determine the distribution of resources to support charitable initiatives. Evaluate the alignment between grant proposals and philanthropic goals, assess impact potential, and make choices that maximize social and environmental benefits. Engage in due diligence and monitor grant outcomes to ensure effective resource allocation.

Applying Decision-Making in Sports Strategy

Sports strategy decisions influence game outcomes and team performance. Analyze opponents, evaluate player capabilities, and make choices that optimize game plans and tactics. Adapt strategies based on real-time assessments and adjust decision-making during gameplay to achieve competitive advantage and success.

Decision-Making in
Digital Transformation

Digital transformation decisions shape the integration of technology in organizations. Assess technological capabilities, consider organizational readiness, and make choices that align with digital transformation goals. Embrace innovation, facilitate change management, and empower employees to adopt digital solutions through effective decision-making.

The Role of Decision-Making in Personal Development

Personal development relies on intentional decision-making to foster growth and self-improvement. Reflect on personal goals, evaluate choices, and make decisions that align with your values and aspirations. Embrace lifelong learning, seek new experiences, and continuously evolve through purposeful decision-making in your personal development journey.

Leveraging Decision-Making in Project Evaluation and Review

Project evaluation and review require effective decision-making to assess project performance and identify areas for improvement. Evaluate project outcomes, analyze data and metrics, and make choices that inform future project planning and execution. Use evaluation results to drive continuous improvement and optimize project outcomes.

Decision-Making in
Social Media Management

Social media management decisions influence brand reputation, audience engagement, and online presence. Evaluate social media platforms, develop content strategies, and make choices that align with brand values and target audience preferences. Monitor social media analytics and adjust decision-making to optimize social media performance.

Applying Decision-Making in
Personal Conflict Resolution

Personal conflict resolution requires skillful decision-making to promote understanding and reconciliation. Assess the root causes of conflict, actively listen to all parties involved, and make choices that prioritize open communication, empathy, and compromise. Strive for win-win solutions and embrace conflict as an opportunity for growth and resolution.

Decision-Making in
Product Development

Product development decisions shape the design, features, and marketing of new products. Conduct market research, assess consumer needs, and make choices that align with market demand and company goals. Balance innovation with feasibility and profitability to drive successful product development outcomes.

The Role of Decision-Making in Talent Acquisition and Management

Talent acquisition and management decisions influence the success and growth of organizations. Evaluate candidate qualifications, assess cultural fit, and make choices that align with organizational values and objectives. Develop strategies for talent retention, career development, and succession planning through effective decision-making in talent management.

Leveraging Decision-Making in Ethical Investing

Ethical investing decisions align financial goals with social and environmental values. Assess investment opportunities, evaluate corporate responsibility practices, and make choices that support sustainable and socially responsible companies. Engage in impact investing and align investment decisions with personal values for positive change.

Decision-Making in
Virtual and Remote Work Environments

Virtual and remote work environments require effective decision-making to foster collaboration, productivity, and work-life balance. Evaluate technology platforms, establish communication protocols, and make choices that support remote team engagement and performance. Embrace flexibility and adapt decision-making to the unique challenges and opportunities of virtual work.

Applying Decision-Making in Competitive Analysis

Competitive analysis decisions drive strategic positioning and market differentiation. Evaluate competitors, assess market trends, and make choices that capitalize on strengths and exploit competitor weaknesses. Develop strategies that maximize competitive advantage through informed decision-making and proactive market analysis.

Decision-Making in
Corporate Governance

Corporate governance decisions ensure transparency, accountability, and ethical practices within organizations. Evaluate governance frameworks, establish board structures, and make choices that promote integrity and shareholder value. Embrace diversity and inclusion in decision-making processes to foster effective corporate governance.

The Role of Decision-Making in Personal Well-Being

Personal well-being relies on intentional decision-making that prioritizes self-care, mental health, and work-life balance. Evaluate personal needs, set boundaries, and make choices that support physical and emotional well-being. Embrace self-reflection and self-compassion as guiding principles for decision-making that enhances personal well-being.

Leveraging Decision-Making in Crisis Communication

During times of crisis, effective decision-making in communication is crucial. Assess the situation, gather relevant information, and make choices that prioritize transparency, empathy, and the well-being of stakeholders. Develop crisis communication plans, anticipate potential challenges, and adjust decisions in real-time to navigate crises successfully.

Decision-Making in
Design Thinking

Design thinking involves making decisions that foster innovation and user-centric solutions. Evaluate user needs, generate creative ideas, and make choices that address user pain points and deliver meaningful experiences. Embrace iteration, collaboration, and empathy as guiding principles for decision-making in the design thinking process.

Applying Decision-Making in Data Privacy and Security

Data privacy and security decisions are essential for protecting sensitive information and maintaining trust with stakeholders. Evaluate data protection measures, assess privacy risks, and make choices that prioritize compliance with privacy regulations and best practices. Develop robust security protocols and proactively address potential vulnerabilities through informed decision-making.

Decision-Making in
Digital Marketing Strategy

Digital marketing decisions shape the effectiveness of marketing campaigns and customer engagement. Evaluate target audiences, analyze market trends, and make choices that optimize digital marketing strategies across various channels. Utilize data analytics and consumer insights to inform decision-making and enhance the impact of digital marketing efforts.

The Role of Decision-Making in Emotional Intelligence

Emotional intelligence involves making decisions that enhance self-awareness, self-regulation, empathy, and interpersonal relationships. Reflect on emotions, assess the impact of choices on oneself and others, and make decisions that prioritize emotional well-being and positive social interactions. Cultivate emotional intelligence through conscious decision-making and continuous self-reflection.

Leveraging Decision-Making in
Green and Sustainable Business Practices

Green and sustainable business practices require informed decision-making to reduce environmental impact and promote social responsibility. Evaluate resource consumption, assess supply chain practices, and make choices that prioritize sustainability, renewable energy, and waste reduction. Embrace circular economy principles and engage in eco-friendly decision-making to drive positive change.

Decision-Making in
Agile Project Management

Agile project management relies on iterative and collaborative decision-making to deliver value in a fast-paced environment. Assess project requirements, prioritize deliverables, and make choices that align with customer needs and project goals. Embrace adaptability and foster open communication to empower teams in agile decision-making processes.

Applying Decision-Making in
Crisis Leadership

Crisis leadership requires effective decision-making to guide teams and organizations through challenging times. Evaluate risks, assess available resources, and make choices that prioritize safety, ethical conduct, and organizational resilience. Communicate transparently, inspire confidence, and adapt decisions as circumstances evolve to navigate crises successfully.

Decision-Making in
Diversity, Equity, and Inclusion

Diversity, equity, and inclusion decisions drive inclusive cultures and equitable practices within organizations. Evaluate policies, assess representation, and make choices that promote diversity, eliminate biases, and foster inclusive environments. Embrace proactive decision-making that respects and values diverse perspectives and experiences.

The Role of Decision-Making in Social Entrepreneurship

Social entrepreneurship involves making choices that address social and environmental challenges while pursuing business goals. Evaluate social impact, assess business viability, and make choices that align with the organization's social mission. Embrace innovation, collaborate with stakeholders, and use business as a force for positive change through intentional decision-making.

Leveraging Decision-Making in Crisis Recovery

Crisis recovery requires strategic decision-making to rebuild, restore, and recover from a disruptive event. Evaluate the extent of the damage, assess available resources, and make choices that prioritize immediate needs and long-term recovery goals. Develop recovery plans, coordinate efforts, and adapt decisions as the situation evolves to facilitate a successful recovery.

Decision-Making in
Global Market Expansion

Global market expansion decisions are crucial for organizations seeking to enter new international markets. Evaluate market potential, assess cultural nuances, and make choices that align with global business strategies. Consider factors such as market research, localization, and regulatory compliance to ensure successful market expansion.

Applying Decision-Making in Humanitarian Aid and Relief Efforts

Humanitarian aid and relief efforts require effective decision-making to provide help to those in need. Assess the scale of the crisis, evaluate resource availability, and make choices that prioritize the well-being and dignity of affected individuals. Collaborate with humanitarian organizations, government entities, and local communities to optimize aid delivery.

Decision-Making in Personal Financial Planning

Personal financial planning relies on intentional decision-making to achieve financial goals and long-term stability. Evaluate income, expenses, and savings objectives, and make choices that align with personal financial priorities. Consider investment options, risk tolerance, and retirement planning to develop a comprehensive financial plan.

The Role of
Decision-Making in Digital Ethics

Digital ethics decisions involve navigating ethical challenges in the digital realm. Evaluate data privacy, algorithmic biases, and the ethical implications of emerging technologies. Make choices that prioritize ethical conduct, digital inclusivity, and responsible use of technology in order to build a digital landscape that benefits society as a whole.

Leveraging Decision-Making in Public Transportation Planning

Public transportation planning requires informed decision-making to improve accessibility, efficiency, and sustainability. Evaluate transportation needs, assess infrastructure options, and make choices that prioritize public safety and environmental impact. Consider factors such as ridership patterns, community input, and technological advancements in transportation planning decisions.

Decision-Making in Personal Goal Setting

Setting and achieving personal goals requires effective decision-making. Reflect on aspirations, evaluate personal strengths and weaknesses, and make choices that align with desired outcomes. Develop action plans, prioritize tasks, and adjust decisions as progress is made towards personal goals.

Applying Decision-Making in Philanthropic Collaboration

Philanthropic collaboration decisions involve partnering with other organizations or individuals to maximize social impact. Evaluate shared goals, assess complementary strengths, and make choices that foster collaboration and enhance collective philanthropic efforts. Embrace strategic partnerships and collective decision-making to drive meaningful change.

Decision-Making in
Political Campaign Strategy

Political campaign strategy decisions shape electoral success and voter engagement. Evaluate target demographics, assess political landscapes, and make choices that optimize campaign messaging, mobilization efforts, and fundraising strategies. Consider public opinion, policy issues, and campaign data to inform decision-making throughout the campaign process.

The Role of Decision-Making in Sustainable Urban Planning

Sustainable urban planning decisions promote environmentally friendly and livable cities. Evaluate land use, transportation options, and energy efficiency measures, and make choices that prioritize sustainability, resilience, and community well-being. Engage stakeholders, consider future growth projections, and embrace innovative approaches to sustainable urban planning decision-making.

Leveraging Decision-Making in Digital Transformation

Digital transformation decisions are critical for organizations to adapt to technological advancements and stay competitive. Evaluate the current digital landscape, assess organizational capabilities, and make choices that prioritize digitalization efforts and customer-centric strategies. Embrace emerging technologies, streamline processes, and foster a culture of innovation through informed decision-making in digital transformation.

Decision-Making in
Public Safety and Emergency Management

Public safety and emergency management decisions play a vital role in protecting communities during crises and ensuring public well-being. Evaluate risks, assess emergency response plans, and make choices that prioritize public safety, effective coordination, and resource allocation. Engage with relevant agencies, collaborate with community stakeholders, and adjust decisions based on real-time assessments to enhance public safety efforts.

Applying Decision-Making in Intellectual Property Management

Intellectual property management decisions involve safeguarding and leveraging intellectual assets for competitive advantage. Evaluate patent and copyright strategies, assess licensing opportunities, and make choices that protect intellectual property rights while maximizing commercialization potential. Stay informed about intellectual property laws and engage legal experts to guide decision-making in intellectual property management.

Decision-Making in
Crisis Prevention

Crisis prevention decisions are proactive measures taken to mitigate risks and avoid potential crises. Evaluate vulnerabilities, assess early warning signs, and make choices that prioritize risk prevention, employee training, and robust crisis management protocols. Foster a culture of risk awareness and proactive decision-making to prevent crises before they occur.

The Role of Decision-Making in Community Development

Community development decisions drive positive social change and empower local communities. Evaluate community needs, assess available resources, and make choices that prioritize inclusivity, sustainability, and economic development. Engage community members, foster partnerships, and employ participatory decision-making processes to enhance community development efforts.

Leveraging Decision-Making in Remote Learning and Education

Remote learning and education decisions have become increasingly important in the face of global challenges. Evaluate technology infrastructure, assess pedagogical approaches, and make choices that optimize remote learning experiences for students. Consider accessibility, student engagement, and support services to ensure equitable and effective remote education through informed decision-making.

Decision-Making in Cybersecurity Risk Management

Cybersecurity risk management decisions are crucial for protecting digital assets and mitigating cyber threats. Evaluate potential vulnerabilities, assess security measures, and make choices that prioritize data protection, threat detection, and incident response. Stay updated on emerging threats, engage with cybersecurity experts, and employ proactive decision-making to safeguard digital environments.

Applying Decision-Making in
Social Media Governance

Social media governance decisions involve establishing policies and guidelines to ensure responsible and ethical social media use within organizations. Evaluate risks, assess content strategies, and make choices that align with organizational values, legal requirements, and user engagement goals. Train employees, monitor social media activities, and adjust decisions to maintain a positive online reputation.

Decision-Making in Disaster Resilience Planning

Disaster resilience planning decisions aim to enhance community resilience and preparedness in the face of natural or man-made disasters. Evaluate hazard assessments, assess infrastructure vulnerabilities, and make choices that prioritize resilience measures, early warning systems, and community engagement. Engage with disaster management agencies, collaborate with stakeholders, and employ evidence-based decision-making in disaster resilience planning.

The Role of Decision-Making in Sustainable Tourism

Sustainable tourism decisions promote responsible travel practices that minimize environmental impact and support local communities. Evaluate destination sustainability, assess tourism development plans, and make choices that prioritize cultural preservation, environmental conservation, and community empowerment. Engage with local stakeholders, adopt sustainable tourism certifications, and employ sustainable decision-making practices to drive positive change in the tourism industry.

Leveraging Decision-Making in Customer Experience Management

Customer experience management decisions are crucial for creating positive interactions and fostering loyalty. Evaluate customer feedback, assess touchpoints, and make choices that prioritize personalized experiences, convenience, and customer satisfaction. Implement customer-centric strategies, leverage technology, and continuously monitor and adjust decisions to enhance the overall customer experience.

Decision-Making in
Disaster Risk Reduction

Disaster risk reduction decisions focus on minimizing the impact of natural and man-made disasters. Evaluate vulnerability assessments, assess risk reduction measures, and make choices that prioritize prevention, preparedness, and resilience. Engage with disaster management agencies, community stakeholders, and employ evidence-based decision-making to effectively mitigate disaster risks.

Applying Decision-Making in
Mental Health Support

Mental health support decisions are critical for promoting well-being and providing help to individuals facing mental health challenges. Evaluate available resources, assess treatment options, and make choices that prioritize accessibility, stigma reduction, and holistic care. Collaborate with mental health professionals, community organizations, and employ empathetic decision-making to support mental health needs effectively.

Decision-Making in
International Development Aid

International development aid decisions aim to address poverty, inequality, and social challenges in developing countries. Evaluate development goals, assess local needs, and make choices that prioritize sustainable development, capacity-building, and social empowerment. Collaborate with local stakeholders, international organizations, and employ participatory decision-making to drive positive change in international development efforts.

The Role of Decision-Making in Technology Ethics

Technology ethics decisions involve considering the ethical implications of emerging technologies. Evaluate potential risks, assess societal impact, and make choices that prioritize ethical use, privacy, and human well-being. Engage in public discourse, advocate for responsible technology practices, and employ ethical decision-making frameworks to navigate the ethical challenges of evolving technologies.

Leveraging Decision-Making in Corporate Culture Transformation

Corporate culture transformation decisions drive positive change within organizations by reshaping values, norms, and behaviors. Evaluate existing culture, assess desired cultural attributes, and make choices that prioritize inclusivity, innovation, and employee well-being. Engage employees, foster leadership commitment, and employ transformative decision-making to create a thriving corporate culture.

Decision-Making in
Personal Conflict Resolution

Personal conflict resolution decisions aim to address interpersonal conflicts and promote peaceful resolutions. Evaluate the root causes of conflicts, assess communication dynamics, and make choices that prioritize active listening, empathy, and constructive dialogue. Embrace conflict as an opportunity for growth and employ empathetic decision-making to resolve conflicts effectively.

Applying Decision-Making in
Sustainable Fashion

Sustainable fashion decisions aim to reduce the environmental and social impact of the fashion industry. Evaluate supply chain practices, assess material sourcing, and make choices that prioritize ethical manufacturing, circular fashion, and conscious consumerism. Engage with sustainable fashion organizations, adopt sustainable certifications, and employ responsible decision-making to drive positive change in the fashion industry.

Decision-Making in
Workplace Diversity and Inclusion

Workplace diversity and inclusion decisions promote equitable and inclusive work environments. Evaluate organizational diversity, assess inclusive policies and practices, and make choices that prioritize diversity recruitment, equal opportunities, and diverse leadership representation. Foster an inclusive culture, engage in unconscious bias training, and employ inclusive decision-making to create a diverse and inclusive workplace.

The Role of Decision-Making in Personal Growth and Development

Personal growth and development require intentional decision-making to foster self-improvement and lifelong learning. Reflect on personal strengths and weaknesses, assess growth opportunities, and make choices that align with personal values and goals. Embrace challenges, seek feedback, and employ intentional decision-making to continuously grow and develop as an individual.

Leveraging Decision-Making in Social Entrepreneurship

Social entrepreneurship decisions drive innovative solutions to social and environmental challenges. Evaluate social impact opportunities, assess business viability, and make choices that prioritize positive change and sustainability. Engage with communities, stakeholders, and employ creative decision-making to create impactful and financially sustainable social enterprises.

Decision-Making in
Crisis Resource Allocation

During times of crisis, resource allocation decisions are crucial to meet urgent needs efficiently. Evaluate available resources, assess demand, and make choices that prioritize equitable distribution and maximum impact. Employ evidence-based decision-making, collaborate with humanitarian organizations, and adjust decisions based on real-time assessments to optimize resource allocation.

Applying Decision-Making in
Health Policy

Health policy decisions play a significant role in shaping healthcare systems and improving public health outcomes. Evaluate health data, assess policy options, and make choices that prioritize equitable access, affordability, and quality of care. Engage with healthcare professionals, policymakers, and employ evidence-based decision-making to develop effective health policies.

Decision-Making in
Cross-Cultural Communication

Cross-cultural communication decisions aim to promote understanding and effective communication across diverse cultural contexts. Evaluate cultural norms, assess communication styles, and make choices that prioritize cultural sensitivity, respect, and inclusivity. Embrace intercultural learning, practice active listening, and employ empathetic decision-making to bridge cultural gaps.

The Role of Decision-Making in Sustainable Agriculture

Sustainable agriculture decisions focus on promoting environmentally friendly and socially responsible farming practices. Evaluate land use, assess farming methods, and make choices that prioritize soil health, biodiversity, and food security. Embrace organic farming, regenerative agriculture, and employ sustainable decision-making to ensure a resilient and sustainable food system.

Leveraging Decision-Making in Digital Accessibility

Digital accessibility decisions aim to ensure inclusive access to digital platforms and technologies for individuals with disabilities. Evaluate accessibility guidelines, assess user needs, and make choices that prioritize accessible design, assistive technologies, and equal digital opportunities. Engage with accessibility experts, conduct user testing, and employ inclusive decision-making to create digitally inclusive environments.

Decision-Making
in Innovation Ecosystems

Innovation ecosystem decisions drive collaboration and innovation within a network of organizations, startups, and institutions. Evaluate partnership opportunities, assess knowledge exchange platforms, and make choices that foster collaboration, knowledge sharing, and technological advancements. Engage with innovation hubs, support startup initiatives, and employ collaborative decision-making to nurture vibrant innovation ecosystems.

Applying Decision-Making in Environmental Education

Environmental education decisions aim to promote awareness and understanding of environmental issues. Evaluate educational approaches, assess curriculum design, and make choices that prioritize experiential learning, sustainability literacy, and active engagement. Engage with educators, develop environmental education programs, and employ learner-centered decision-making to empower individuals to become environmental stewards.

Decision-Making in
Remote Team Management

Remote team management decisions are critical to foster productivity and collaboration in distributed work environments. Evaluate communication tools, assess team dynamics, and make choices that prioritize effective communication, team cohesion, and individual well-being. Foster a remote-friendly culture, empower team members, and employ adaptive decision-making to successfully manage remote teams.

The Role of Decision-Making in Ethical Leadership

Ethical leadership decisions shape ethical conduct and values within organizations. Evaluate ethical dilemmas, assess moral principles, and make choices that prioritize integrity, fairness, and ethical decision-making. Lead by example, foster ethical cultures, and employ ethical decision-making frameworks to inspire ethical behavior and guide organizational success.

Leveraging Decision-Making in Renewable Energy Transition

Renewable energy transition decisions play a vital role in combating climate change and promoting sustainable energy sources. Evaluate renewable energy options, assess feasibility studies, and make choices that prioritize clean energy generation, energy efficiency, and carbon reduction. Engage with renewable energy experts, collaborate with stakeholders, and employ strategic decision-making to drive successful renewable energy transitions.

Decision-Making in
Ethical Supply Chain Management

Ethical supply chain management decisions aim to ensure responsible sourcing, fair labor practices, and environmental stewardship throughout the supply chain. Evaluate supplier practices, assess sustainability certifications, and make choices that prioritize transparency, human rights, and social responsibility. Engage with suppliers, conduct regular audits, and employ ethical decision-making to build ethical and sustainable supply chains.

Applying Decision-Making in Urban Mobility Planning

Urban mobility planning decisions focus on creating efficient, sustainable, and inclusive transportation systems in urban areas. Evaluate transportation infrastructure, assess mobility patterns, and make choices that prioritize multimodal transportation, accessibility, and reduced emissions. Engage with urban planners, transportation experts, and employ data-driven decision-making to develop effective urban mobility plans.

Decision-Making in
Personal Time Management

Personal time management decisions are crucial for individuals to optimize their productivity and work-life balance. Evaluate tasks and priorities, assess time commitments, and make choices that prioritize goal achievement, self-care, and personal well-being. Develop time management strategies, embrace productivity tools, and employ self-discipline to make the most effective use of time.

The Role of Decision-Making in
Green Building Design

Green building design decisions focus on creating environmentally friendly and energy-efficient buildings. Evaluate sustainable design principles, assess green building certifications, and make choices that prioritize energy conservation, indoor air quality, and sustainable materials. Engage with architects, engineers, and employ sustainable decision-making to create eco-friendly and sustainable buildings.

Leveraging Decision-Making in International Trade and Globalization

International trade and globalization decisions shape economic growth, international relations, and market integration. Evaluate trade agreements, assess market opportunities, and make choices that prioritize fair trade, sustainable development, and inclusive growth. Engage with trade experts, collaborate with global partners, and employ strategic decision-making to navigate the complexities of international trade and globalization.

Decision-Making in
Personal Financial Investments

Personal financial investment decisions are critical for long-term financial growth and security. Evaluate investment options, assess risk tolerance, and make choices that align with financial goals and values. Conduct thorough research, seek professional advice, and employ informed decision-making to build a diversified and successful investment portfolio.

Applying Decision-Making in Healthcare Innovation

Healthcare innovation decisions drive advancements in medical technology, patient care, and healthcare delivery. Evaluate innovative solutions, assess patient needs, and make choices that prioritize patient safety, cost-effectiveness, and improved health outcomes. Engage with healthcare professionals, collaborate with innovators, and employ evidence-based decision-making to foster healthcare innovation.

Decision-Making in Circular Economy Transition

Circular economy transition decisions aim to promote resource efficiency and reduce waste in economic systems. Evaluate product lifecycle, assess recycling, and reuse opportunities, and make choices that prioritize product design, waste reduction, and closed-loop systems. Engage with sustainability experts, collaborate with stakeholders, and employ circular decision-making to transition to a more sustainable and circular economy.

The Role of Decision-Making in Interpersonal Relationships

Interpersonal relationship decisions shape the dynamics and quality of relationships with others. Evaluate communication styles, assess personal boundaries, and make choices that prioritize empathy, trust, and effective communication. Foster active listening, embracing emotional intelligence, and employ respectful decision-making to cultivate healthy and meaningful interpersonal relationships.

Leveraging Decision-Making in
Social Impact Investing

Social impact investing decisions aim to generate both financial returns and positive social or environmental impact. Evaluate investment opportunities, assess impact measurement frameworks, and make choices that align with social and environmental goals. Engage with impact investing organizations, conduct due diligence, and employ impact-focused decision-making to drive sustainable and socially responsible investment practices.

Decision-Making in Cybersecurity Governance

Cybersecurity governance decisions focus on establishing policies and practices to protect digital assets and information systems. Evaluate cybersecurity frameworks, assess risk management strategies, and make choices that prioritize data privacy, incident response, and regulatory compliance. Engage with cybersecurity professionals, conduct regular audits, and employ proactive decision-making to ensure robust cybersecurity governance.

Applying Decision-Making in
Disaster Recovery and Reconstruction

Disaster recovery and reconstruction decisions play a crucial role in rebuilding communities after a disaster. Evaluate infrastructure damage, assess community needs, and make choices that prioritize resilient infrastructure, community engagement, and social equity. Collaborate with disaster recovery agencies, involve community members, and employ inclusive decision-making to facilitate effective recovery and reconstruction efforts.

Decision-Making in Personal Health and Wellness

Personal health and wellness decisions are vital for maintaining a balanced and healthy lifestyle. Evaluate lifestyle choices, assess nutrition, and exercise habits, and make choices that prioritize physical and mental well-being. Embrace preventive care, practice mindfulness, and employ self-care decision-making to nurture personal health and wellness.

The Role of Decision-Making in Innovation Leadership

Innovation leadership decisions drive a culture of innovation within organizations. Evaluate market trends, assess technological advancements, and make choices that prioritize creativity, collaboration, and risk-taking. Foster a supportive environment, encourage idea generation, and employ visionary decision-making to inspire innovation and drive organizational growth.

Leveraging Decision-Making in Environmental Impact Assessment

Environmental impact assessment decisions are crucial for evaluating the potential environmental consequences of development projects. Evaluate project plans, assess ecological impacts, and make choices that prioritize environmental conservation, sustainability, and social responsibility. Engage with environmental experts, involve local communities, and employ informed decision-making to minimize negative environmental impacts.

Decision-Making in
Team Diversity and Inclusion

Team diversity and inclusion decisions aim to create diverse and inclusive work environments that foster innovation and collaboration. Evaluate team composition, assess inclusion practices, and make choices that prioritize diversity recruitment, equal opportunities, and inclusive team dynamics. Foster a culture of belonging, embracing diverse perspectives, and employ inclusive decision-making to harness the benefits of team diversity.

Applying Decision-Making in Crisis Communication and Reputation Management

Crisis communication and reputation management decisions are critical for maintaining trust and managing public perception during challenging times. Evaluate crisis scenarios, assess stakeholder concerns, and make choices that prioritize transparency, empathy, and timely communication. Develop crisis communication plans, engage with stakeholders, and employ strategic decision-making to protect and enhance organizational reputation.

Decision-Making in
Sustainable Tourism Development

Sustainable tourism development decisions focus on promoting tourism practices that minimize environmental impact and benefit local communities. Evaluate tourism development plans, assess cultural preservation strategies, and make choices that prioritize sustainable tourism practices, community involvement, and responsible travel. Engage with tourism stakeholders, adopt sustainable tourism certifications, and employ sustainable decision-making to foster sustainable tourism development.

The Role of Decision-Making in Personal Relationship Building

Personal relationship building decisions play a vital role in establishing and nurturing meaningful connections with others. Evaluate personal values, assess communication styles, and make choices that prioritize authenticity, empathy, and active listening. Cultivate trust, foster open dialogue, and employ relational decision-making to build and maintain healthy and fulfilling personal relationships.

Leveraging Decision-Making in Agile Leadership

Agile leadership decisions are essential for navigating rapidly changing business environments and fostering adaptability. Evaluate market trends, assess organizational capabilities, and make choices that prioritize flexibility, collaboration, and continuous improvement. Empower teams, embrace iterative decision-making, and foster a culture of agility to drive organizational success.

Decision-Making in
Crisis Mental Health Support

Crisis mental health support decisions focus on providing immediate assistance and intervention during mental health crises. Evaluate crisis intervention strategies, assess available resources, and make choices that prioritize empathy, safety, and effective communication. Collaborate with mental health professionals, engage in crisis response training, and employ compassionate decision-making to support individuals in crisis.

Applying Decision-Making in
Human Rights Advocacy

Human rights advocacy decisions aim to promote and protect fundamental human rights and dignity. Evaluate human rights issues, assess advocacy strategies, and make choices that prioritize inclusivity, equity, and social justice. Engage with human rights organizations, collaborate with impacted communities, and employ strategic decision-making to drive impactful human rights advocacy.

Decision-Making in
Personal Skill Development

Personal skill development decisions are critical for continuous learning and professional growth. Evaluate skill gaps, assess learning opportunities, and make choices that prioritize skill acquisition, practice, and mastery. Embrace lifelong learning, seek mentorship, and employ deliberate decision-making to enhance personal skills and competencies.

The Role of Decision-Making in Social Media Influencing

Social media influencing decisions involves building a personal brand and engaging audiences on social media platforms. Evaluate target audience preferences, assess content strategies, and make choices that prioritize authenticity, value creation, and responsible influencing. Engage with followers, analyze social media analytics, and employ strategic decision-making to become an impactful social media influencer.

Leveraging Decision-Making in Project Portfolio Management

Project portfolio management decisions focus on aligning project investments with organizational goals and maximizing returns. Evaluate project portfolios, assess resource allocation, and make choices that prioritize project selection, risk management, and strategic alignment. Employ portfolio analysis techniques, engage with stakeholders, and employ data-driven decision-making to optimize project portfolio performance.

Decision-Making in
Community Engagement and Empowerment

Community engagement and empowerment decisions aim to foster participatory decision-making and amplify community voices. Evaluate community needs, assess engagement strategies, and make choices that prioritize inclusivity, collaboration, and community capacity-building. Embrace community-led initiatives, involve diverse stakeholders, and employ democratic decision-making processes to empower communities.

Applying Decision-Making in Nonprofit Governance

Nonprofit governance decisions focus on ensuring accountability, transparency, and effective management within nonprofit organizations. Evaluate governance structures, assess compliance with regulations, and make choices that prioritize ethical conduct, mission alignment, and stakeholder engagement. Engage with nonprofit governance experts, adopt best practices, and employ strategic decision-making to strengthen nonprofit governance.

Decision-Making in
Digital Transformation Governance

Digital transformation governance decisions are crucial for overseeing and managing digital initiatives within organizations. Evaluate digital transformation strategies, assess risks and opportunities, and make choices that prioritize digital ethics, data privacy, and digital capability development. Engage with digital transformation experts, collaborate with stakeholders, and employ effective decision-making to drive successful digital transformation initiatives.

The Role of Decision-Making in Sustainable Development Planning

Sustainable development planning decisions aim to balance economic, social, and environmental considerations for long-term prosperity. Evaluate development goals, assess environmental impact assessments, and make choices that prioritize sustainable resource management, social equity, and resilient infrastructure. Engage with sustainable development experts, involve local communities, and employ integrated decision-making to drive sustainable development planning.

Leveraging Decision-Making in Ethical AI Development

Ethical AI development decisions focus on ensuring the responsible and unbiased use of artificial intelligence technologies. Evaluate AI algorithms, assess potential biases, and make choices that prioritize fairness, transparency, and accountability. Engage with AI ethics experts, conduct ethical reviews, and employ ethical decision-making frameworks to develop AI systems that benefit society.

Decision-Making in
Disaster Preparedness Planning

Disaster preparedness planning decisions are critical for proactively mitigating the impact of potential disasters. Evaluate potential risks, assess preparedness measures, and make choices that prioritize early warning systems, emergency response protocols, and community education. Collaborate with disaster management agencies, engage with local communities, and employ evidence-based decision-making to enhance disaster preparedness.

Applying Decision-Making in
Public Health Emergency Response

Public health emergency response decisions aim to protect public health and mitigate the spread of infectious diseases. Evaluate disease outbreaks, assess public health interventions, and make choices that prioritize timely communication, resource allocation, and evidence-based interventions. Collaborate with public health experts, engage with stakeholders, and employ agile decision-making to effectively respond to public health emergencies.

Decision-Making in Personal Leadership Development

Personal leadership development decisions are crucial for enhancing leadership skills and effectiveness. Evaluate leadership strengths and weaknesses, assess developmental opportunities, and make choices that prioritize self-awareness, continuous learning, and personal growth. Engage in leadership training, seek mentorship, and employ reflective decision-making to cultivate strong leadership capabilities.

The Role of Decision-Making in Sustainable Business Practices

Sustainable business practices decisions aim to minimize environmental impact and promote social responsibility within organizations. Evaluate business operations, assess sustainability metrics, and make choices that prioritize environmental stewardship, social equity, and responsible supply chain management. Engage with sustainability experts, adopt sustainable certifications, and employ sustainable decision-making to drive positive change in business practices.

Leveraging Decision-Making in Financial Risk Management

Financial risk management decisions are critical for minimizing financial losses and ensuring stability within organizations. Evaluate financial risks, assess risk tolerance, and make choices that prioritize risk mitigation, financial resilience, and regulatory compliance. Engage with financial experts, employ risk analysis techniques, and employ informed decision-making to effectively manage financial risks.

Decision-Making in
Public Policy Formulation

Public policy formulation decisions shape government policies and regulations that impact society. Evaluate policy options, assess stakeholder perspectives, and make choices that prioritize the public interest, social justice, and evidence-based decision-making. Engage with policy experts, consult with impacted communities, and employ democratic decision-making processes to develop effective public policies.

Applying Decision-Making in Ethical Journalism

Ethical journalism decisions focus on upholding journalistic integrity, accuracy, and responsible reporting. Evaluate news sources, assess journalistic standards, and make choices that prioritize objectivity, fairness, and accountability. Engage in ethical discussions, adhere to professional codes of conduct, and employ ethical decision-making to uphold the principles of ethical journalism.

Decision-Making in
Conflict Resolution and Mediation

Conflict resolution and mediation decisions aim
to facilitate peaceful resolutions to interpersonal or
organizational conflicts. Evaluate conflict dynamics,
assess communication barriers, and make choices that
prioritize effective communication, active listening,
and compromise. Engage in conflict resolution training,
embrace alternative dispute resolution techniques, and
employ neutral decision-making to foster positive conflict
resolution outcomes.

The Role of Decision-Making in Personal Well-being and Work-Life Balance

Personal well-being and work-life balance decisions are crucial for maintaining physical, mental, and emotional health. Evaluate personal priorities, assess work demands, and make choices that prioritize self-care, boundary setting, and work-life integration. Embrace self-reflection, practice stress management techniques, and employ intentional decision-making to nurture personal well-being and achieve work-life balance.

Leveraging Decision-Making in
Social Innovation

Social innovation decisions drive transformative solutions to address societal challenges and create positive social impact. Evaluate social issues, assess innovative approaches, and make choices that prioritize collaboration, scalability, and sustainability. Engage with social innovation networks, involve diverse stakeholders, and employ creative decision-making to foster social innovation and drive positive change.

Decision-Making in
Data Privacy and Protection

Data privacy and protection decisions are critical for safeguarding personal information and ensuring compliance with privacy regulations. Evaluate data handling practices, assess privacy risks, and make choices that prioritize data security, transparency, and user consent. Engage with data privacy experts, implement privacy protocols, and employ ethical decision-making to protect individuals' privacy rights.

Applying Decision-Making in Ethical Consumerism

Ethical consumerism decisions involve making conscious purchasing choices that align with personal values and support ethical and sustainable practices. Evaluate product origins, assess supply chain transparency, and make choices that prioritize fair trade, environmental sustainability, and social responsibility. Engage in ethical consumer research, support ethical brands, and employ informed decision-making to promote ethical consumerism.

Decision-Making in
Cultural Heritage Preservation

Cultural heritage preservation decisions aim to protect and conserve historical and cultural landmarks and artifacts. Evaluate cultural significance, assess preservation methods, and make choices that prioritize conservation, public access, and community engagement. Collaborate with cultural heritage experts, involve local communities, and employ sustainable decision-making to ensure the preservation of cultural heritage for future generations.

The Role of Decision-Making in Resilient Leadership

Resilient leadership decisions focus on navigating challenges, fostering resilience, and leading with adaptability. Evaluate situational demands, assess team dynamics, and make choices that prioritize agility, emotional intelligence, and employee well-being. Foster a resilient culture, embrace learning from failures, and employ decisive decision-making to lead effectively in times of uncertainty.

Leveraging Decision-Making in Community-Based Disaster Risk Management

Community-based disaster risk management decisions involve empowering communities to actively participate in disaster preparedness and response efforts. Evaluate community needs, assess local resources, and make choices that prioritize community engagement, capacity-building, and sustainable risk reduction measures. Collaborate with community leaders, involve local organizations, and employ participatory decision-making to enhance community resilience.

Decision-Making in
Personal Ethical Dilemmas

Personal ethical dilemma decisions involve navigating complex moral situations and making choices aligned with personal values and principles. Evaluate ethical considerations, assess potential consequences, and make choices that prioritize integrity, empathy, and moral reasoning. Reflect on ethical frameworks, seek guidance from trusted advisors, and employ conscientious decision-making to navigate personal ethical dilemmas.

Applying Decision-Making in Entrepreneurial Ventures

Entrepreneurial venture decisions drive the establishment and growth of new businesses. Evaluate market opportunities, assess business models, and make choices that prioritize innovation, market fit, and sustainable growth. Engage with entrepreneurial networks, seek mentorship, and employ calculated decision-making to launch and scale successful entrepreneurial ventures.

Decision-Making in
Sustainable Waste Management

Sustainable waste management decisions aim to reduce waste generation, promote recycling, and minimize environmental impact. Evaluate waste management practices, assess recycling infrastructure, and make choices that prioritize waste reduction, circular economy principles, and responsible waste disposal. Engage with waste management experts, involve local communities, and employ sustainable decision-making to achieve sustainable waste management goals.

The Role of Decision-Making in Conflict Transformation

Conflict transformation decisions focus on fostering positive change and promoting peaceful resolutions in situations of conflict. Evaluate conflict dynamics, assess root causes, and make choices that prioritize dialogue, reconciliation, and long-term peacebuilding. Engage in conflict resolution training, embrace restorative justice approaches, and employ transformative decision-making to facilitate conflict transformation.

Leveraging Decision-Making in
Digital Marketing Strategies

Digital marketing strategies decisions play a vital role in reaching and engaging target audiences in the digital landscape. Evaluate market trends, assess audience preferences, and make choices that prioritize personalized messaging, data-driven insights, and omni-channel marketing approaches. Engage with digital marketing experts, analyze performance metrics, and employ strategic decision-making to drive successful digital marketing campaigns.

Decision-Making in
Sustainable Forest Management

Sustainable forest management decisions focus on balancing economic, environmental, and social aspects of forestry. Evaluate forest ecosystems, assess logging practices, and make choices that prioritize forest conservation, biodiversity protection, and sustainable timber production. Collaborate with forestry experts, involve local communities, and employ adaptive decision-making to ensure the long-term sustainability of forests.

Applying Decision-Making in
Gender Equality Initiatives

Gender equality initiatives decisions aim to promote equal rights and opportunities for all genders. Evaluate gender disparities, assess policy frameworks, and make choices that prioritize gender mainstreaming, equal representation, and empowerment. Engage with gender equality advocates, collaborate with stakeholders, and employ intersectional decision-making to drive meaningful progress in achieving gender equality.

Decision-Making in Workplace Safety and Health

Workplace safety and health decisions are crucial for creating safe and healthy work environments. Evaluate workplace hazards, assess safety protocols, and make choices that prioritize employee well-being, accident prevention, and compliance with occupational health and safety regulations. Engage with safety professionals, conduct risk assessments, and employ proactive decision-making to ensure a safe working environment.

The Role of Decision-Making in
Global Climate Change Mitigation

Global climate change mitigation decisions aim to reduce greenhouse gas emissions and combat climate change. Evaluate carbon footprints, assess mitigation strategies, and make choices that prioritize renewable energy adoption, energy efficiency, and sustainable transportation. Engage with climate change experts, collaborate with international organizations, and employ ambitious decision-making to contribute to global climate change mitigation efforts.

Leveraging Decision-Making in Social Impact Measurement

Social impact measurement decisions involve evaluating the effectiveness and outcomes of social initiatives and programs. Evaluate impact measurement frameworks, assess data collection methods, and make choices that prioritize meaningful metrics, stakeholder engagement, and continuous learning. Engage with impact measurement experts, involve impacted communities, and employ evidence-based decision-making to assess and improve social impact.

Decision-Making in
Personal Goal Setting and Achievement

Personal goal setting and achievement decisions are crucial for personal growth and success. Evaluate aspirations, assess goal feasibility, and make choices that prioritize clarity, motivation, and actionable steps. Develop goal-setting strategies, track progress, and employ disciplined decision-making to effectively achieve personal goals and aspirations.

Applying Decision-Making in
Digital Privacy Education

Digital privacy education decisions focus on promoting awareness and responsible use of personal data and online privacy. Evaluate educational approaches, assess curriculum development, and make choices that prioritize digital literacy, data protection, and online safety. Engage with privacy advocates, collaborate with educators, and employ learner-centered decision-making to empower individuals with digital privacy knowledge.

Decision-Making in
Sustainable Water Resource Management

Sustainable water resource management decisions aim to ensure equitable access to clean water while preserving water ecosystems. Evaluate water availability, assess conservation strategies, and make choices that prioritize water efficiency, water quality preservation, and community engagement. Collaborate with water management experts, involve local stakeholders, and employ integrated decision-making to achieve sustainable water resource management.

The Role of Decision-Making in Resilient Urban Planning

Resilient urban planning decisions focus on creating cities that can withstand and recover from shocks and stresses. Evaluate urban vulnerabilities, assess infrastructure resilience, and make choices that prioritize disaster preparedness, climate adaptation, and social inclusivity. Engage with urban planning experts, involve local communities, and employ forward-thinking decision-making to build resilient and sustainable cities.

Leveraging Decision-Making in Corporate Social Responsibility

Corporate social responsibility decisions aim to integrate social and environmental considerations into business practices. Evaluate social and environmental impacts, assess stakeholder expectations, and make choices that prioritize responsible sourcing, employee well-being, and community engagement. Engage with sustainability experts, collaborate with stakeholders, and employ ethical decision-making to drive impactful corporate social responsibility initiatives.

Decision-Making in Sustainable Fashion and Apparel Industry

Sustainable fashion and apparel industry decisions focus on promoting environmentally and socially responsible practices within the fashion industry. Evaluate supply chain practices, assess material sourcing, and make choices that prioritize circular fashion, fair labor, and waste reduction. Collaborate with fashion industry stakeholders, embrace sustainable certifications, and employ conscious decision-making to drive sustainable transformation in the fashion industry.

Applying Decision-Making in
Mental Health Advocacy

Mental health advocacy decisions aim to raise awareness, reduce stigma, and improve access to mental health support. Evaluate mental health needs, assess advocacy strategies, and make choices that prioritize education, advocacy campaigns, and policy reform. Engage with mental health experts, collaborate with advocacy organizations, and employ compassionate decision-making to advance mental health advocacy efforts.

Decision-Making in
Sustainable Tourism Destination Management

Sustainable tourism destination management decisions focus on promoting responsible and sustainable tourism practices. Evaluate destination resources, assess carrying capacity, and make choices that prioritize community involvement, cultural preservation, and environmental conservation. Engage with tourism stakeholders, involve local communities, and employ destination-based decision-making to create sustainable and resilient tourism destinations.

The Role of Decision-Making in Artificial Intelligence Governance

Artificial intelligence governance decisions aim to address the ethical, social, and legal implications of AI technologies. Evaluate AI applications, assess ethical frameworks, and make choices that prioritize transparency, accountability, and human rights. Engage with AI ethics experts, collaborate with policymakers, and employ inclusive decision-making to govern AI technologies responsibly.

Leveraging Decision-Making in
Philanthropic Investments

Philanthropic investment decisions involve strategically allocating resources to maximize social impact. Evaluate philanthropic goals, assess project proposals, and make choices that prioritize measurable outcomes, sustainability, and long-term systemic change. Engage with philanthropic advisors, conduct impact evaluations, and employ strategic decision-making to drive transformative philanthropic investments.

Decision-Making in Personal Conflict Resolution

Personal conflict resolution decisions aim to navigate and resolve conflicts in personal relationships. Evaluate communication dynamics, assess underlying issues, and make choices that prioritize empathy, active listening, and effective problem-solving. Embrace conflict resolution techniques, seek mediation if needed, and employ empathetic decision-making to promote understanding and resolution.

Applying Decision-Making in Energy Transition Planning

Energy transition planning decisions focus on shifting towards renewable and sustainable energy sources. Evaluate energy systems, assess technological advancements, and make choices that prioritize renewable energy adoption, energy efficiency, and grid integration. Engage with energy experts, collaborate with stakeholders, and employ data-driven decision-making to drive successful energy transition planning.

Decision-Making in Corporate Governance and Ethics

Corporate governance and ethical decisions shape ethical conduct and accountability within organizations. Evaluate governance structures, assess ethical guidelines, and make choices that prioritize transparency, integrity, and responsible decision-making. Foster an ethical culture, establish ethical frameworks, and employ ethical decision-making practices to ensure sound corporate governance.

The Role of Decision-Making in Social Justice Advocacy

Social justice advocacy decisions aim to address systemic inequalities and promote equitable opportunities for marginalized communities. Evaluate social justice issues, assess advocacy strategies, and make choices that prioritize inclusivity, equity, and empowerment. Engage with social justice activists, collaborate with community organizations, and employ intersectional decision-making to drive impactful social justice advocacy.

Leveraging Decision-Making in Sustainable Agriculture

Sustainable agriculture decisions focus on promoting environmentally friendly and socially responsible practices within the agricultural sector. Evaluate farming methods, assess soil health, and make choices that prioritize organic farming, biodiversity conservation, and responsible water management. Collaborate with agricultural experts, embrace sustainable certifications, and employ regenerative decision-making to drive sustainable agriculture practices.

Decision-Making in
Ethical Leadership

Ethical leadership decisions involve making choices that prioritize integrity, fairness, and ethical conduct in leadership roles. Evaluate ethical dilemmas, assess ethical frameworks, and make choices that prioritize ethical decision-making, transparency, and accountability. Engage in ethical leadership training, seek guidance from ethical mentors, and employ principled decision-making to lead with integrity.

Applying Decision-Making in Disaster Risk Reduction

Disaster risk reduction decisions aim to minimize the impact of disasters on communities and promote resilience. Evaluate disaster risks, assess risk reduction strategies, and make choices that prioritize early warning systems, community preparedness, and infrastructure resilience. Collaborate with disaster management agencies, involve local communities, and employ proactive decision-making to enhance disaster risk reduction efforts.

Decision-Making in Accessible Technology Design

Accessible technology design decisions focus on creating inclusive and user-friendly products and services. Evaluate accessibility needs, assess design guidelines, and make choices that prioritize universal design, usability, and accessibility standards. Engage with accessibility experts, involve users with diverse abilities, and employ user-centered decision-making to create technology that is accessible to all.

The Role of Decision-Making in Community Empowerment

Community empowerment decisions aim to foster self-sufficiency, active participation, and collective decision-making within communities. Evaluate community needs, assess capacity-building strategies, and make choices that prioritize empowerment, inclusivity, and sustainable development. Engage with community organizers, collaborate with local leaders, and employ participatory decision-making to drive community empowerment initiatives.

Leveraging Decision-Making in Ethical Supply Chain Management

Ethical supply chain management decisions aim to ensure responsible sourcing, fair labor practices, and environmental sustainability throughout the supply chain. Evaluate supplier practices, assess sustainability certifications, and make choices that prioritize transparency, human rights, and social responsibility. Engage with suppliers, conduct regular audits, and employ ethical decision-making to build ethical and sustainable supply chains.

Decision-Making in Personal Financial Planning

Personal financial planning decisions are critical for achieving financial goals and long-term financial security. Evaluate income, expenses, and financial goals, and make choices that prioritize budgeting, savings, and investment strategies. Seek financial advice, conduct regular financial assessments, and employ prudent decision-making to create a sound personal financial plan.

Applying Decision-Making in Public Art and Cultural Initiatives

Public art and cultural initiatives decisions aim to enhance community identity, cultural expression, and public spaces. Evaluate community interests, assess artistic proposals, and make choices that prioritize cultural diversity, artistic excellence, and community engagement. Collaborate with artists, involve community members, and employ inclusive decision-making to drive impactful public art and cultural initiatives.

Decision-Making in Sustainable Transportation Planning

Sustainable transportation planning decisions focus on creating efficient, accessible, and environmentally friendly transportation systems. Evaluate transportation infrastructure, assess mobility patterns, and make choices that prioritize public transit, active transportation, and reduced emissions. Engage with urban planners, transportation experts, and employ data-driven decision-making to develop sustainable transportation plans.

The Role of Decision-Making in Personal Growth and Development

Personal growth and development decisions are crucial for continuous learning, self-improvement, and personal fulfillment. Evaluate personal aspirations, assess development opportunities, and make choices that prioritize self-reflection, goal setting, and skill building. Embrace lifelong learning, seek personal growth resources, and employ intentional decision-making to foster personal growth and development.

Leveraging Decision-Making in Digital Citizenship

Digital citizenship decisions involve responsible and ethical behavior in the online world. Evaluate digital platforms, assess online interactions, and make choices that prioritize digital literacy, online safety, and respectful communication. Engage in digital citizenship education, promote positive online engagement, and employ critical decision-making to foster a healthy and inclusive digital community.

Decision-Making in
Sustainable Packaging Solutions

Sustainable packaging decisions aim to reduce the environmental impact of packaging materials and waste. Evaluate packaging materials, assess lifecycle assessments, and make choices that prioritize recyclability, renewable resources, and minimal packaging waste. Collaborate with packaging experts, embrace sustainable packaging certifications, and employ innovative decision-making to drive sustainable packaging solutions that minimize environmental harm.

Conclusion

In this text, a man takes drastic measures to destroy his car, but then later saves it to showcase his success. He emphasizes the importance of making decisions, stating that cleaning up a list of decisions can provide inspiration for years to come. The man also highlights the power of desire, mentioning that it often waits for a trigger to ignite it. He advises welcoming all experiences and not building walls that can hinder happiness. Lastly, he talks about the significance of resolve, defining it as promising oneself to never give up.

The text encourages persistence and determination, using the analogy of a baby learning to walk. It suggests that we should continue pursuing our goals until we achieve them, no matter how long it takes. The author believes that by paying the price of persistence, we can uncover life's greatest treasures. Overall, the text emphasizes the importance of making decisions, having strong desires, embracing experiences, and staying resolved in the face of challenges. It encourages readers to never give up and to keep pushing forward until they achieve their desired outcomes.

The power of decisions is undeniable. Each choice we make shapes our journey and determines the quality of our lives. By embracing the process of decision-making, staying true to our values, and persisting through challenges, we unlock our true potential and create a life filled with purpose, growth, and fulfillment.